Me No Habla
With Acento

Me No Habla With Acento

Contemporary Latino Poetry

edited by
EMANUEL XAVIER

This book has been published by El Museo del Barrio
in collaboration with Rebel Satori Press

Cover and interior artwork by Juan Betancurth
Book design by Riley Hooker

ISBN: 978-1-60864-039-3

Printed in the U.S.A.

REBEL SATORI PRESS   EL MUSEO DEL BARRIO
P.O. Box 363   1230 Fifth Avenue at 104th St.
Hulls Cove, ME 04644   New York, NY 10029
www.rebelsatoripress.com   www.elmuseo.org   (212) 831 7272

Library of Congress Cataloging-in-Publication Data

Me no habla with acento : contemporary Latino poetry / edited by Emanuel Xavier.
    p. cm.
  Includes bibliographical references.
  ISBN 978-1-60864-039-3 (pbk.)
  1. American poetry--Hispanic American authors. 2. American poetry--21st century.
I. Xavier, Emanuel.
  PS591.H58M4 2010
  811'.6080868--dc22
                         2010029507

PUBLICATION CREDITS

Grateful acknowledgment is made to the following publications in which these poems first originally appeared:

Edwin Torres: "I'm Trying To Perfect My Assent" first appeared in *XCP #20*, 2008 (Cross-Cultural Poetics). "The Intermission Clown" first appeared in *Yes Thing No Thing*, 2010 (Edwin Torres, Roof Books).

Nancy Mercado: "The Dead" and "In My Perfect Puerto Rico" first appeared in *Black Renaissance Noire* Magazine, 2010 (New York University). "Milla" first appeared in *ALOUD: Voices from the Nuyorican Poets Cafe*, 1994 (Henry Holt). "On My Return from Puerto Rico to the U.S. or (the Idleness of It All)" first appeared in *In Defense of Mumia*, 1996 (Writers and Readers). "No Nothin" first appeared in *It Concerns the Madness*, 2000 (Longshot Productions).

Urayoán Noel: "Foray" first appeared in *Sous Rature, Issue #3*, Summer/Fall 2009. "Beached Wail" first appeared in *5AM*, Fall 2009. "Nobody Home" first appeared in *Acentos Review*, Spring 2010. "Manco Munidades" first appeared in *Boringkén*, 2008 (Urayoán Noel, Ediciones Callejón, San Juan, PR).

Sheila Maldonado: "Pool" first appeared in *Poetry in Performance*, The City College of New York, 2003. "At the Meer in Harlem" first appeared in *The Portable Boog Reader 4*, 2010.

Lisa Alvarado: "Bashert" is an excerpt from *Raw Silk Suture*, 2008 (Floricanto Press).

Jason "Majestik Originality" Hernandez: "For Her" and "Took Your Seat" first appeared in *Verses/Poetry (Inside the Mind of an Emcee/Poet)*, 2009 (CreateSpace).

CONTENTS

SIN PELOS EN LA LENGUA

Writing an introduction for this anthology has been quite a dare. Perhaps it is because experience has taught me there is absolutely no way one person could ever speak for an entire community. Within the modern day Latino/a poetry scene in the United States, the only genuine commonality shared is that we live in a country where we are all still a minority. We share our truths creatively using English, Spanish, and/or Spanglish words to paint our canvas for an insatiable audience longing to find themselves somewhere between the sentences in our poems.

To mainstream America and the United States census, we are all the same except for maybe different shades of skin color. To those who have a better grasp of reality, we encompass diverse cultures, beliefs, and maybe even accents. We all strive to be loved, respected, and heard within the realms of the American dream and, as poets, we allow ourselves the permission to challenge and create dialogue as we capture the world around us with metaphors or slang.

The word *poetry* itself derives from Greek origin and the Latin word *poeta,* which means *poet.* Nonetheless, however evocative or lyrical we might strive to be, America has simply cast us off as Chicano or Nuyorican poets or spoken word artists and boxed us away into niche markets without much regard for the rich mosaic that form our great oral tradition.

Much has been written about the notable contributions of Pablo Neruda, Federico García Lorca, Jorge Luis Borges, and other poets who wrote in Spanish and whose works were translated into English and other languages. For the world at large, it is perhaps more complex to embrace contemporary Latino American poetry because it is a mash up of languages, vernaculars, and styles. Whereas in other countries most people speak more than one language, living in a country where most believe English-only is the way to go has nurtured a more rebellious and "edgy" aesthetic to our verse.

The work of Edwin Torres, Pedro Pietri, Cherríe Moraga, Miguel Algarin, Sandra Maria Esteves, Raul Salinas, and other iconic modern day Latino poets is therefore more uncompromising and reflective of what we have been subjected to as a community. In order for us to reach our youth and bring poetry into their lives as a more accessible art form, some of us have embraced elements of hip hop while others have become storytellers and yet we have all taken on the role of teachers somewhere along the way.

This collection is a celebration of just a handful of the many talented and promising Latino poets that have emerged in the United States. The poems you are about to read are the result of migration and years of challenges.

These words cannot be boxed or checked off in a single category because we are all influenced by the world around us and, in most of the United States, the world around us consists of diversity. We are a product of our society with an understanding of what our parents taught us about our backgrounds.

We rhyme and we don't. While most would rather cast us as formidable speakers at cafes and bookstores, I give thanks to El Museo del Barrio for acknowledging our art as poets and spoken word artists.

This book is a testament to the many contributions of our people to this nation, and one of hopefully more opportunities for us to be heard louder than ever before on our own terms- with freedom and *orgullo en el corazón, siempre.*

—Emanuel Xavier, Editor

HYPER-HYBRIDIZED CUMBIAELECTRONICA BACHATA-HOP BEATS

Nuyorican poetry and El Museo del Barrio were born around the same time—parallel gritos demanding that Latino art in New York should be seen and heard.

By the 1960's, a generation of Puerto Rican workers had already lived out their adult lives in the city, and birthed children who had no recollection of the island's sights, sounds and smells. These children began to create poetry, paintings, and performance art out of their big-city experience. At the same time, those who remembered la isla worked to preserve the often-overlooked legacy of its artists— poets like Julia de Burgos, Pedro Pietri, and Clemente Soto Vélez, and artists like Rafael Tufiño, Marcos Dimas or Carlos Osorio.

The epicenter for this Nuyorican arts movement was the East Harlem neighborhood of El Barrio. In 1969, Raphael Montañez Ortiz, with the help of community leaders, teachers, and local families, founded El Museo del Barrio as a platform for the Puerto Rican art that was then invisible in the city's major museums. For the first time, New York's children could see at El Museo that our people painted, drew, and sculpted, and had been doing this for millennia. That same year, the homegrown revolutionaries known as the Young Lords illegally took over the neighborhood's First Spanish Methodist Church to set up breakfast and education programs for local families. In that church, Nuyorican poet Pedro Pietri performed the searing debut of his Puerto Rican Obituary—a classic that went on to inspire countless other young Latino poets. As Urayóan Noel once said, "Until Pedro Pietri, I didn't know we wrote."

Out of this rich shared history, El Museo and the Nuyorican poetry scene evolved along similar paths. Both have grown to embrace not only Puerto Rican artists, but also the incredible variety of Latinos who have since arrived in the city, from Sephardic Jewish Argentines to Afro-Dominicans to Mexican mestizos.

As third, and even fourth, generation Latinos mingle with recién llegados in this constantly shifting global crossroads, Latino visual artists and spoken word poets are now spawning work that speaks three or more languages and sings to hyper-hybridized cumbiaelectronica bachata-hop beats.
As identities become even more hyphenated and our cultures absorb each other, it's no surprise the line between visual arts and poetry has also blurred allowing for the rise of performance art, a major part of El Museo's programming. At the same time the definition of art museum has evolved as well, with the expansion of El Museo's public programs – including poetry and literary series among others.

In recent years, El Museo has taken an active role in the city's poetry scene. Through our monthly Speak Up! spoken word poetry series, we've hosted spoken word artists including this collection's editor, Emanuel Xavier; and contributors Edwin Torres, Caridad de la Luz ("La Bruja"), Rigoberto González, Urayoan Noel, Frank Pérez, and Roberto "Simply Rob" Vassilarakis, among many others. Starting in 2007 with a single poetry evening at the museum, we now present eight spoken word programs per year, with about five poets performing at each one—plus open mic sessions where new poets are welcome. We've also begun a series of poetry-writing workshops for youth, led by the Peace Poets and La Bruja. And in our permanent collection exhibition celebrating our 40th anniversary, we've included a live video of Pedro Pietri performing at the Young Lords' church. History comes full circle, here, in the neighborhood where the whole revolú began.

It only makes sense, then, that El Museo should present *Me No Habla With Acento*. This, our first venture into publishing poetry, is just the natural evolution of 40 years of Latino visual art and poetry growing up together in New York. To paraphrase Pedro Pietri, "here we come, here we come, donde our roots are from." Enjoy!

—Gonzalo Casals
Director of Education and Public Programs,
El Museo del Barrio

Cheeseburger in Paradise, 2010
Mixed media collage

Edwin Torres

ME NO HABLA SPIC

i remember one afternoon in soho
sitting on the sidewalk
with my longhaired cat, harry
single and carefree
showing my beautiful pet to the world
people passing by, saying
what a cute spic

i remember my first day of my first job after college
running to catch the subway
wearing a maroon vest on a spring morning
passing under a pigeon's butt
dropping a wet one on my back, giving me
an aura i'd never live up to, people whispering on the platform,
what a cute spic

i remember my first poem
at an open mike, the host
announcing my name among the many
the crowd holding their applause
the bartender, the muse in the bathroom
the clergy at the front table, gathered in judgment
of a cute spic

i remember my first connection
between artifice and libido after my first show and tell
weaving that tendril of libertine inhalation
through the temporary airspace of second grade
my wet-spot palpable, little Veronica in polka dots
playing horsie with my hankie, thinking
what a cute spic

i remember the late night drink
set-up by the
morning phone call on tenth street & avenue a
playing strip scrabble
on PCP, running out of letters
before socks, until the only words left were
what and cute

i remember my first assignment to compose a lecture
as a visiting professor, choosing as my topic
the apparent-only-to-me similarities between futurism's early fulcrum
    parades
and the first migration of nuyoricans, prompting the class
    to pick through the paper's remains, leaving no grace or misguided
    flower child unlit
which subsequently sparked the chair of the department down from
    her throne
to admonish, why bother with spic when the sixties have passed

i remember the city i love
reflected in plate glass
on a monday morning in midtown
jackhammers and blue skies
pierced though Chrysler, scraping miles
above the seething rush, breathless and barking
in unison, what a cute spic

i remember having the chance
to perform for the king
and my drummer using lipstick
to write a message on the king's giant ass
while i kept dancing, the audience
howling in underwear
that matched the failure of a cute spic

i remember a girl with my last name
who came up to me after a show
to tell me how
lots of people with my last name were watching me now
and that i needed to be responsible now
all the while me looking at her legs
thinking, what a cute spic

i remember my sisters
teaching me how to dance salsa
when i was in junior high
the hips following an island i'd never been on
excuse me, politely holding my hand out,
could I have this dance, my sister playfully
responding, why yes you cute spic

i remember holding an umbrella for Debbie
in 7th grade after a dance
waiting for the bus, my first act
of chivalry before acne
the hot girl in class, under my umbrella
not looking or saying a word, on a rainy school night, but i'm sure
thinking, what a cute spic

i remember my uncle
taking me to cover a wedding, my main job
to hold the flash and eat free food
his humor continuing through the music that looked
and tasted like butter or was that cheese
on the car ride back, laughing non-stop at his own puerile stream
and me thinking, what a cute spic

i remember the audience levitating
in the middle of a poem
just one mic on a slightly raised platform and me
shapeshifting through eyesight, the sound out of my pupils
blurred in an ocean of green effervescent inertia, the shapeless horde
hovering through the unbelievably intact embryonic fluid
of a star cluster's dna spiral, my spic-ness re-sourced
as kinetic quasars through light years of fragile diplomacy
thinking, it doesn't get any spic'er than this

i remember re-reading every email i sent
to feel as if i were the person
receiving my own words, basking in their clever reach
to feel the warmth of many messages
from many people, all of them me
a conglomerate of sinewy desperation
wrapped up in the viral opportunity of a cute spic
i remember that time in the mailroom
after months of talking a good game
finally having to prove
that of course i'd done it before, the cleaning lady
walking in on bone and flesh,
carpet burns and saran, oh...excuse me,
wrap, is that your...oops, what a cute...whoah

i remember the need to keep secrets
and hold onto something
that no one else had, just to own something,
until my tummy hurt
and the stain that followed explained
a backlog of excess discolored by the lifelong
incineration of a cute spic

i remember performing a butoh dance
wearing nothing but a thong and black body paint,
an enigma hiding in full view
my older girlfriend's friend in the audience
confirming hydraulic suspicion
both of them
nodding, cute and hmmm

i remember changing the light bulb
for a smaller girl on the lower e
my long frame standing on a wooden crate
after a few bong hits, her hands
holding me steady by the hips
my belt lined-up with her brow, her lips
mouthing out, wota keyute spike

i remember skinny-dipping
in an ocean after a reading and thinking
this feels great but first I need to get a reading
near an ocean for this to ever happen
as the naked yoga doppelganger compared tree
postures in the moonlight to my exposed id
while remaining balanced by the chant of speak with spic
i remember being trapped
by stanza and convention
where words had been withdrawn
from the vault of language i maintain
as an obelisk for rhizomic displays
of rendered territory flared into the stigma
of a tediously benign cute spic

i remember getting 50 cents
stolen from me by the bully
down the block, seeing an easy mark

in high-water pants with freshly bought Matchbox racer
held tight in my pocket, praying
he wouldn't force my hands out, laughing, as i walked off
to his bully friend, yo spic you think that's cute, punch

i remember being seduced
by the stage
wearing industrial foam on my head
while a ping-pong ball
made its way from throat to hand
as my disembodied voice emerged through my rectum
offering the boatman's dilemma, how much for a cute spic

i remember running from a mouse
into the beehive
of a pajama party cross-town
slipping under the covers
before knowing what to do there
spooning in the wrong position while
fingering the button of a cute spic

i remember waking up one morning
from uneasy dreams and finding myself
transformed in my bed
into a giant cucaracha helpless on my back
draped under a flag of colors and shapes
i couldn't pronounce, my mom opening the shutters
letting the sun in, singing, oh what a beautiful spic
i remember the best of times
the worst of times, the age of wisdom
the age of foolishness, the epoch of disbelief, the season
of hope, the winter of despair, the morning of cocochi, having
everything before us, nothing direct to heaven
going the other way in short…the noisiest authority insisting
on the superlative degree comparable only to the tale of a cute spic

i remember the conceit of discovering
a catch-phrase built around identity
and how fleeting the prospect
of a fused mass, guided by skincolor before brainpower
the astral dimensions inherent
in a dna of parable presenting the overwhelming

differences that claim how the one is cute before the one is spic

i remember finding a banana peel
under a year's worth of newspapers, my refrigerator
duct-taped shut so i wouldn't be tempted to store even more
unopened containers and my sports jacket
ironed along a complication of creases to better present an
immaculately pressed emblem of normalcy
to the world outside my congested walls, what, a cute, spic

i remember meeting the person i would spend my life with
and not knowing until years later
that i knew my life had just been completed
the first moment our eyes met
but not knowing that moment would not be realized
until many years after, lost in the time travel of love's engaged mess
by sonatas both cute and incomplete

i remember thinking i needed a format
to contain my writing and in the process
stumbling upon a giant machine that would one day
dictate to the world how to think and compose
sentences by stealing what had been written
and rearranging a sense of magnificence with a sense
of boredom into the, by now, stock regurgitations of a cute spic
i remember sitting in soho
with my two-year old son
surrounded by expensive buildings
where there used to be none, the world passing
me, just thankful to get some rest
in the sun's imperfections, the people
ooh'ing and ahh'ing…what a cute spic

I AM TRYING TO PERFECT MY ASSÉNT

I'd like to sliver A-mer-ica
live in a separate A-mer-ica
one that is more of a-ME-rica
the one that I don't THAT'S America

Entering the USA
Leaving *la isla* behind
Leaving The Atlantic behind
        (the Atlantic *culito*...if you will)
Limping into America's horizon
        (all these ways are ways of same)

America waiting for us
open arms joweled with expectation
and furry eyebrows, dismantling
her strip mall hairdos

Havana No Seño or
Negila or Negril
Gi'tude — but not me...

    BIENVENUDO
        TO THE BICOASTAL LENGUA!

Forked tongue mandala — speech so true
splits the tongue...
into bi-coastal lesions
as America tries hard to perfect her ASS-ent...her AC-cent!

    (*oye Sombra...wheng deed my Other bekom djur Other?*)

    Tongue-iva
    Lady Saliva
    Mounted Imbiber
    Ridin the rider

    but no one rides wit me
        'cuz I'm wit me
            and I ain't no one
                see, we all wanna piece o'dat *lengua*

Syllables caught on her ear
　　　　screaming echolia for the *PaPa-patria*
melt down your moetrics *MaMa-mantra*

Lip-piss-sizing on her back legs, America
　　　　rears up and proudly mounts
Rapunzel's locks, casas blancas, ivory torres, ebonic flores,
　　　　　　edwín porés — open your bordés
　　　　　　and call me you — I'm another taino
　　　　　　reachando — por tu

O lonely widow of vari-coastal impunity
　　　　safe against your bargain culture, illegally
aliened by the color of grass — how ironic...
　　　　to gain freedom...
　　　　you must acquire a card...
　　　　the color of nature...

　　　O Merdre-Rica
　　　O Mer Rica
　　　O Sea of Rich Chica-CACA
　　　O-WHO-sica
　　　O-YOU-sica
　　　OHMMMM-MALAVA
　　　PALA-BRAVA...MU-sica

　　　O-CooCOOM-bia
　　　Hum-BOMB-bia
　　　Afri-SUM-pica
　　　Come-COME, miha
　　　O-MA-MA-rica
　　　O-PA-PA-rica
　　　O-WHO-WHO-sica
　　　O-YOU-YOU-sica
　　　OH...　　　*I wanna mix-up a-mer-ica*
　　　　　　　　live in the other a-mer-ica
　　　　　　　　maybe discover a-ME-rica
　　　　　　　　because I'm alone...I'm America

FATHER TO FATHER

it has been too long
since I've seen my father's grave
I can remember the grass,
its shape, the weeds spelling out
how long it's been

I can smell the flowers
left by my aunt
reminding me how she visits
with a frequency
any brother would cherish

the row of tombstones
the cars passing by
the umbrellas when I was little
the cake and coffee at
grandma's house afterwards

I can sense the desperation
as I walk between the rows
on top of graves
searching for where I thought he was
once again

am I trying to live through you
imagining you as I could never be
is this what I need to resolve
before becoming a father
before the legacy you've left me takes root

let's have a talk pop
when you left
I barely had a grip on what you were
what I'd become
and I'm still that boy imagining himself a man

but what is that supposed to be
pops, what does it mean to say *man*?
is your legacy pride disguised
as machismo, the conflict

of the new age Puerto Rican

why don't you let me find you
there are beautiful people
who find themselves trapped
and no matter how often
they are told how beautiful they are

never believe it
until one day it happens
and that self-worth
is what completes them
and I don't know

if it's you or me that needs to be told
but one of us is beautiful
so just let me find you
I've met men who have shown me
heard their conversations

seen apparitions, witnessed the actions
of what would form a father figure
put all that together in my head
and still I find myself
tripping over something that used to be there

let me find you
maybe you're hiding
maybe you do need to be told
maybe what it comes down to
is you and me

talking man to man
whatever that means to you

THE INTERMISSION CLOWN

The man, the woman, the dog, the ball.
The black man, the white woman, the black dog, the red ball.
Not once did I mention
the relationship between the man and the dog.

Never the lover, the ball. Nor the woman kiss
the man before the ball returned by dog.
Nor did I bother with waves, or ocean
or beach. The sun hitting the hair of the woman.

As the man came close to her cheek. The dog
caught in the sun, by the ball's
returning gaze. Never do we learn
how intimate the man has been

with the woman or the dog. How long
have they been in each other's lives, arms. What is the ball's
relationship to the dog, to the color. New or favorite.
The same could be said as red.

And not once have I mentioned if the dog belongs
to the woman or the man or the black or the beach.
And the woman, trying to escape the man's
grasp. And this, a prelude to a breakup

in a matter of minutes. The ball in the red mouth
a transition in orbit. The shoreline baked
in golden sandstorms. Blue waves
on a fading shift of ardent erosion.

Nor do we smell the way they both
ignore the dog. Joyously retrieving the ball
from the ocean. And what about
the manner in which this viewer came upon them.

How I used walk to cross
that part of the telling. That obvious alert
into when we enter, and when we go.
The porous weight that follows echo.

Trailing talk behind each tiny summit of rock,
strewn with reminders of what belongs together.
Catching the size of sirens before they drift apart.
The travel to never-be in the giant size of things.

Never did I mention, how they all tried to become
the other. The man, the woman, the woman, the man.
The dog, the ball, the ball, the dog. The secret
of each other's knowing. The red, the black, the white, the gold,

unearthed in my viewing. Nor did I allow my witness
a true flight. A risen consequence from the pit
of what I brought with me. My history attached to theirs,
in alignment with my telling.

And when did I leave out how I left. Where,
in this story, is the time or position of the shoreline's
pass. Every change affecting its greeting.
Each wave, another frame, another stone.

And in what I've just told you
did I ever mention thought
or gift or carnival. The horizon's volume
relived as a tremor, doing its vertical remember in you.

Its impulse for legs, to stand apart
from perspective and light.
To walk
in the telling of things.

BIT BY BITE

Fuzz or static
choose one, eight hours earlier
and I will live your stream —
the sleep you swim in
entire fields of feedback
prophesized as hair

Windswept across sierra
plateaus submerged by sandmen
and water saints, Isadora's virgins —
Goya's Saturn
carnivorous father hands me
clear strokes to behave

As one would
if drenched by howling dunes
across ancient bones —
ambient feathers
on daughters the size of fireworks
dormant water bombs

Gathered by feral tomorrows
what's worse, a nation without a sun
or a moon —
that's easy, no moon
without a sun
you only live in the dark

Which is blood
when slammed against
fly or mosquito —
penetrate sublimity
through a mask of light
disguised as sweep

What is haze or fuzz to you
will someday ride the bare back
of all your moonlit swims —
a silhouette of elegiac serenades
curved along a color
dreamed eight hours ago

Rigoberto González

ANXIETY GALLERY

Portrait One: Rebel Shot Through the Eye

A bullet displaces the eyeball. It pierces
whatever it sees. My son, keep away
from broken glass, his mother used to plead.
And when she bows to bless him, the dead man shatters
her teeth. Now, she speaks through the asshole
of her lips, her tongue a mole that quivers at
the smallest hint of light. Unmoved, the son locks
his face to the sky as his mother fans the fire
on her jaw, yearning to kiss the next passerby.

Portrait Two: Decomposition Cycle

Bald chickens roam the dumping grounds.
They've pecked each other's combs off
and are angered by their ugly skulls.
What better comfort than pinching the pimples
off the hands that no longer feed them.
When the flesh slips off, the birds panic
at the sight of chicken bones. What betrayal
to be tricked into becoming cannibals again.
Worms boil in their stomachs clenched like fists.

Portrait Three: The Colonel Smoking on the Balcony

The tobacco is Cuban. The pipe fibula.
The dogs disguise themselves as mud
and will be spared the spit. Fireworks tonight—
Chinese ingenuity, American artistry.
The whole town comes out of hiding
now that the houses are gone. The show
begins: when the church explodes, children
scream; when the car explodes, children run;
when the children explode—

GILA

It's no curse
    dragging my belly across
        the steaming sand all day.
    I'm as thick as a callus
        that has shorn off its leg.

If you find me I can explain
    the trail made by a single limb.

        I'm not a ghost.
Don't be afraid.

Though there are ghosts here—
    they strip down to wind
        or slump against rock to evaporate.

Sometimes I crawl beneath the shedding,
backing up into the flesh pit for shade.
    Praise the final moisture of the mouth, its crown
        of teeth that sparkles with silver or gold.

I make a throne of the body
    until it begins to decay.

        And then I'll toss the frock--
death by hunger, death by heat--
    off the pimples of my skin.

    Don't you dare come into my kingdom,
peasant, without paying respect on your knees!

    What generous act did I commit
in my previous life, that I should be
        rewarded with this paradise:

a garden in which every tree that takes root here
    drops its fruit eye-level to me.

MORTUI VIVOS DOCENT

I

In the trunk, a blouse with breasts, a skirt
stretched open by hips that have shaken off
the last whiff of talcum powder at the pothole.
Clumsy dancer, dropping her shoe somewhere between
Mexicali and Calexico. If she were breathing
she'd let the whiskey tell the tale,
sultry syllable after sultry syllable—sí, mi amor.
Mummies are this century's mermaids,
rattling songs that will stop a heart. If we let them,
says the whale-eyed sailor, hands cuffed
to the steering wheel, mumbling the madness
of a man who found a woman whistling
beneath a Mexican moon—music so pretty
he just had to keep it from ruining the terrorist world.

II

This is how you ruin the terrorist world:
cut out the yellow heart of heaven,
drop the bloodless stars into the sea,
blind the women who sit to wonder on the shore.
I knew such a woman. I've kept her comb in my purse
after all these years, since the night my father found her
walking home from the Cachanilla hills.
You know the names, El Abanico, El Dollar, La Puta Eva
y El Pinche Adán, places so plump with pleasure
even the air turns to stupor, drunk with a sensory coma.
Clarification: she was not the body in the ruby corset,
not behind the pair of tassels, not inside the scent
of tangerines. My mother was the mop and bucket
wiping off the fingerprints on the promiscuous wall.

III

This is how you press against the promiscuous wall:
drill the pair of diamonds on your back and moan;

hold your breath, float face-down on the vertical pool;
sway with the shadows set in motion by a swinging
chandelier—an angry father come to claim his child.
He did not catch me then, but he caught me
walking home, my knees still numb from dancing
with the men who love their mamacitas pink
and puckered as if they're sipping wine transparent
as the cloth across their thighs. What could I do
with lips like mine but kiss or whistle loud enough
to be the visible woman my overworked mother
never was? So, papi, keep your only son holy as you stuff
me in the trunk: I'm wearing mother's blouse, mother's skirt.

LA PELONA AS BIRDWOMAN

Tonight
I dared to crawl
beneath the sheets

to be nailed down
around me,
waiting for my lover, she

who enters
without knocking, she
who will unstitch

my every seam
along my thigh,
my side, my armpit.

She who carves
a heart out of the heart
and drops it

down her throat.
Sweet surrender this
slow death in sleep

as I dream
the love-making
is autopsy. How else

will I be hers
completely? Be her
treasure box I said:

a trove of pearls
and stones, the ding
of coins cascading

through her fingers.
The bird over her shoulder
not a parrot, but an owl

to be my mirror
when I close my eyes
and shape a moon-white

bowl out of my face
where she can wash
the hooks of her caress.

Still with water, I'm
one more thing to penetrate.
I'm one more spill

of secrets on the floor.
A puddle glowing green—
she doesn't have to be a sleuth

to see I've taken
all the anti-freeze.
A puddle thick with red—

she'll kneel
next to my wounds
and pray for me,

a string of pigeon skulls
her rosary.
By dawn our bone pièta

breaks out of its shadow,
unleashes its cicada cry.
My daughters drag

their bodies, bruised as bats,
out to the light
and burst in flames

like marigolds.
The crows will leap
down from the trees

to pick them clean.
And my beloved bride,

beloved wife, will laugh

until it hurts her teeth.
It's the feather
of her tongue—

eleventh finger—
I recall
and not the catheter

while the priest recites
his holy dribble
and the churchyard

worker takes a leak.
My sons hold up
their chins with pride

that they have done
their part to hide
my suicide:

they've clipped
my fingertips
to lose the track

back to my prints.
But my beloved knows:
she crouches

on the highest branch
and drops an egg
that cracks my coffin.
Concussion light
squirms through
and I'm in heaven once again—

those times
we screwed like hen
and rooster: I

the squawking chicken

blacking out, and she
the hammering cock.

MORIBUND TRIPTYCH

(left panel)

Agony in the light bulb as you lick your dry teeth,
watching the crows on the wallpaper. In evidence
every failure visible: shoes that have lost not one
but both feet to the crows on the wallpaper;
a belt that couldn't rope the belly in; two nickels
and a penny that missed the last pocket to the street.
On the dresser, a dead man's wallet and the useless
black hole of its mouth. Your children mock you
from the wallet's window, pretending a prison
like the crows on the wallpaper. Your wife
is nowhere to be found. No use looking around.
She has tired of waiting, she has turned
toward the switch, she's out like the crows.
The room deflates, kicking up dust through your
hollow throat. And then not a sound. Not a cough.
Not even skid marks in the fury of escaping crows.

(center panel)

Apples know this truth: skin and muscle soften
into the edible bruise. And then the strange comfort
of surrender. If anyone can bite you anymore she will
want revenge for the brutal surface of your hands
and how they could pry anything open—sealed door,
clamped knees, stubborn hinge of the jaw. Weakling,
even the orchids can bully you now. They crush
their blossoms against your cheek and won't
let you see past them. A warden in white rushes in
on the hour and plunges his knife in your arm.
In another world you could out-blade him with
the razors in your rage, but not in this one, where
your throat won't release its spit-bubble or whimper.
Even the chair dragging its club foot complains
louder than you. The window claims all the attention
when it undoes its housecoat in the morning. Petty
thief every bird that picks at the sill and takes
a piece of your will to trap it behind your teeth.

Little do any of them know that you are simply biding
your time in this disguise. Deflated, your viscera will
swell like sausages. You keep a secret: beneath
the sheets, you grow tumescent-tough, assailant-mean.

    (right panel)

A birthmark creeping up your face.
If we had mouths, we'd kiss it, but the gods who made us
gave us windows through which everything escapes.
The last man who loved us flew out like a sink
and he took the entire kitchen with him.
Let us fondle your mole like a wet papaya seed
and we'll build something bigger, beautiful, and black—
an avocado with a bubble of gold instead of a testicle.
In autumn, we grow fingertips and the tulips change back
to the poor white roots that growl like scars.
And the spidering commences: leaf crawling after leaf.
We will remember you each time a cricket
because its chirp is another small thing we can't hold.
And though the gods who made us gave us legs
we are like chairs to be weighed down into place.
We travel nonetheless. When you sleep we move
into darkness; when you dream we hide among objects.
When you die we walk you through the funnels
of final song. Let us know when you finish
making pumice from the beehive of your heart
and we'll teach you how to burn the bed from the inside out:
from the wood a casket, from the sheets a shroud,
from the flesh a million cherries on the ends of cigarettes.

María Rodríguez-
Morales

I KNOW WHERE I'M AT . . . TELL ME WHERE I'M FROM

I know where I'm at/Brooklyn bred by way of East New York
A Puerto Rican/Nuyorican/Latina/married /mother of four
But tell me where I'm from/ oblige me a bit more
That rich port/that we've been taught/
Christopher Columbus founded
The land where Africanos were enslaved and bounded/
Where woman were scarce in a land so rich/
Tainas y Africanas were added to the mix/
And thus this beautiful spectrum of color/
Los blanquitos/negritos/ my brown sisters and brothers
Descendants transcend cultural boundaries/
They transport me to my past/
I have come to ask/ almost afraid to admit
That I was once immune to my history and its indigenous inhabitants
I've searched for answers/ in lessons/ that schools didn't teach
Two stepping to Salsa beats/front to back/side to side/
the rhythm moving my feet
Hector Lavoe/ Willie Colon/ El Gran Combo
Lechones/bendiciones/y baños de flores
The Saturday/ before the Puerto Rican Day Parade/
Cars of all types/would line up Broadway/
El ritmo de mi país /blaring from every speaker/
Horns honking/flags waving/mi isla bonita
And I felt alive/my heart overflowing with pride/
But once the sea of flags /that lined Fifth Ave/ were all gone/
A part of me died/
My identity was compromised/ by MTV/
Fly jewelry/dope kicks/French tips
And yet I didn't know shit/
Who were our heroes/our influential peoples/I wanted to know/
This is when I discovered Pedro Pietri/Tato Laviera/Miguel Piñero
Julia de Burgos/José de Diego /Lolita Lebron
Just some of the Boricuas who paved the way/
for some of my faves today/
Caridad de La Luz/Flaco and Lemon Anderson
Years have passed/I am a mother of four boys/
who will become four men/
And I am determined to teach them/what I didn't know then/
It's a shame/ how these kids nowadays/ know more/

about pop culture than our culture
And the history of our people/ whom have opened the doors/
I have a personal mission/ myself/for my sons/
And when I am done/ they will know where they're at/
but also, where they're from

RAINBOWS

My mother taught me that rainbows are beautiful.
They signify COURAGE in the eye of aversion
She in her Teflon exterior
Impenetrable
Stalwart
Yet ever so graceful
And I worry that courage does not equal strength
Strength is what you need when you are being attacked
Fear is what I felt thinking of that
My mother taught me that rainbows are beautiful
They signify tolerance in a world of narrow mindedness
Narrow Minded Mess
And I wonder how WE tolerate their blindness
Indifference
When bruises are not exposed on bare fleshy skin
When hurt is etched in memories within
When you are made to believe you are living in sin
When the one place we hold sacred
Is molesting our kin
But you are made to believe you are living in sin.
And I worry, that maybe my patience has run thin.
And I worry if change doesn't come
It may never happen
My mother taught me that rainbows are beautiful
That Stone Walls were created as building blocks
That those blocks built a bridge
A bridge to UNITE
A community enriched with veracity and PRIDE
And I worry
That many have died 'cause they had too much pride
Yet their souls have reincarnated into a Warriors CRY
They tell us Stone Wall was the beginning
A battle not fought is one worth not winning
And so I STAND
My mother taught me that rainbows are beautiful
Her flag is my own.

BABY BLUES

Statistics concluded by ChildHelp.Org

-Almost five children die everyday because of child abuse. More than three out of four are under the age of four.
-It is estimated that between 60-85% of child fatalities due to maltreatment are not recorded as such on death certificates.
-A report of child abuse is made every ten seconds.
-Child abuse occurs at every socio-economic level, across ethnic and cultural lines, within all religions and at all levels of education.
-About 30% of abused and neglected children will later abuse their own children, continuing the horrible cycle of abuse.

I am a miracle
A gift of life
Brought into this world to fulfill dreams
I've yet to have.
I am the future
If I can make it past the present.
Other innocents like me, remain remnants of the past
Victims of ANGER/RESENTMENT/IGNORANCE.
We make the front pages of your Daily News
Another baby found LIFELESS/NEGLECTED/ABUSED.
We don't have a voice
but our cries can be heard through
project courtyards/ stairwells in buildings/ manicured lawns on picket fenced
suburbs.
I do not know RACE
I do not know PLACE
I do not know CLASS
I have become the face of CIRCUMSTANCE
Born to the young mother who yearns for lost adolescent years
Born to the teenage father/born to the streets
Born to the mother, who like me,
always gets beat
born to the fatherless father
born to the uneducated/underpaid/overwhelmed/underprivileged mother
born to the impatient father
born to the mother who has everything,
but I wasn't in the cards mother

born to the father who doesn't want to be tied down . . .
who wants to be free
born to the mother who regrets having me.
I am the mistake that nobody wants
so a cry/spilled milk/soiled diaper
leads to me getting stomped
cracked ribs
broken limbs
black and blues
emaciated bodies from too little food.
Screams for Mercy fall on deaf ears
getting involved is everyone's fear
So I am left to pay for society's excuse,
as I become the headline generated for tomorrow's news

MY NEIGHBORHOOD

Outside, pants and shirts dance
in the gentle breeze
hung to a clothesline
connecting tenement windows.
A labyrinth of sorts
on display for all to see
Tar on the pavement glistens under the ardent heat
BOUNCE. DRIBBLE. SLAM
goes the basketball
through a milk crate
nailed
to the trunk of a tree
POP. SMACK. SLAP
goes the handball against the brick wall
of an adjacent building
SCRAPE. SCRAPE. SCRAPE
goes the piragua man
as he sings his daily jingle
CHERRY. TAMARINDO. COCO. CREMA
He competes with Doña Lola
who sells her own concoction of
coconut ices
the real deal
for a mere .25 cents
Life is sweet
cars drive by with the boomin' systems
boys ride bikes with precious cargo on their pegs
Girls strut to the bodega
for blow pops
jolly ranchers
salt and vinegar chips
quarter waters
an all day excursion
hoping to catch the eye of a potential suitor
king pine y cloro
waft out of apartment windows
strong enough to burn nose hairs
but I am used to it by now
Salsa y merengue blast from speakers
the streets are a musical

inviting me to dance
Woman in rolos
gather on the stoop
a bonchinchar con los vecinos
Old men jovially slap dominoes
on a homemade table of Formica and wood
brown paper bagging
CHUCHAZO!
There is LAUGHTER
There is LIFE
There is LOVE
There is PRIDE
in my neighborhood

Erik "Advocate of Wordz" Maldonado

LIE WITH ME

I HATE ... when you stare at me
Without Emotion
Without a WORD
Your quiet silence
would irritate the most conservative of librarians

SPEAK!!!
Dwell on the silliest of things,
walk me through run on sentences
make me the direct cause of why they cut your cell phone off
and repeat it all tomorrow.
Just,
Lull me to sleep.

I don't wanna see it coming,
Lie up until the end.
Tell me our relationship was sent to a farm upstate
so it could have more room to grow.
Wait until time and maturity give me distance between
the illusion and reality
bliss and truth
us and death
till we part,
lie with me.
Fight for the covers
but let go of the clothes
and the armor.

Lie with me,
Tell me the dog ate the rings,
aliens kidnapped your heart,
and convince me that you kissed him
because you were momentarily blind and he wears the same cologne as me.
Lie with me
In my bed,
share the experience of a drive-in dream,
park in my arms during nightmares
and sleep in a space with a headrest that won't brake.
Lie with me,
because you can't hear the bird's chirping in the morning

until I brush the hair off the side of your head,
and you hate when people hear or read poems I write about you
so to avoid all that you should just,
LIE WITH ME
on top of pillows and below cherry trees
LIE WITH ME
stay near me and ease me with
lies . . . with me
for better or worse
vow to forever lie
your unwanted clothes in my house
so I can assume you will be back.

Don't brush me away,
keep your comb on my bathroom sink,
leave your lipstick in my dresser drawer
and promise me we'll have make-up sex tomorrow

Lie with me,
because I can't stand the truth,
if you're leaving.

MARCH 4TH, 1992

March 4th, 1992
feels like everyday to me.

Last night I was a 12 year old too consumed
with his video games
to spend time with his grandmother.
A bedridden woman
whom just 6 months prior
was making me stuffed shells and brownies.

The old soul whose conservative ways
kept me in line but whose liberal love
fed my spirit. I've always wondered
what I would've said
or done, if I knew you weren't going to wake up the next morning.

I play out in my head
that I'd share one last dream with you,
I'd explain how the boogie man and the monsters in my closet
left me alone because they knew
you were protecting me
and how the doorway to your house
filtered out my insecurities.

But,
I probably would've just cried.

You were the first piece of my heart I had to bury.
I'd like to believe you can hear me.
I wish you the power of x-ray vision
so you can see how my DNA strands
twist and turn
the way your cursive writing did.
I'm just waiting for a sign,
a text message or voicemail
letting me know that you knew
how much I appreciated everything
you've ever done
I need you to know that oxygen doesn't smell the same
and the colors of the world have faded in the wash of my tears.

Memories of you have yet to dry
though I tumble through them like a dryer.
Yeah, they're warm,
always warm.

I can make it in this world without Nintendo,
I can wake up tomorrow morning
without the Sun but, if I'm ever to open my eyes again,
if I'm ever to instill and trust love again,
I need to know you're there.

My smile is in foreclosure,
because I can never pay you back.
You're my first and last poem.
One step behind you,
a million miles away from everything else.

March 4th, 1992 feels like everyday to me.
The day you passed away
and someone hit
the reset button
on my life.

GRAND BATTEMENT EN AVANT

In high school,
I opted to take modern dance and ballet
class over gym.

While my boys ran, lay up drills and suicides,
I Plié'd and Relevé'd.
During lunch I got giggled on,
thoroughly questioned
and unknowingly shunned.
I remained shut.
Confined to a secret; I did not trust
the public's hands
with the bones in my closet.
I was happy with who I was,
felt I had a grand battement en avant
over them all.

Midway into the semester,
the truth came out.
While Mrs. Jordan
had the class practicing lifts,
one of my boys from b-ball practice
walked by the dance studio
and peered in.

There I was,
in navy blue sweat pants
and a white T,
sweating, breathing hard
catching and juggling 30 females in tights.

Young, agile and tangible angels at my sole disposal
I knew me being the only guy in the class
meant me being everyone's partner.
My Fouetté was tight!

I learned the Cat's Claw
while Michelle's thigh gripped my waist.
Mastered the floor work
behind Tina's spot on the mat

and gleefully threw my back out
while practicing the Grand Jeté with Daisy.

Needless to say,
I went from being assumed as being homosexual
to viewed as an ingenious pervert.
2 weeks later, I transferred out,
and spent the rest of the year
trying to box out
shirtless guys,
for a rebound.
How masculine of me.

ON THE SIXTH DAY

"Ya' know Erik,"
my mother begins
her testament.

She confesses her understanding
that I'm getting older
and my body is creating urges.

We only had another block
to go before reaching church.
I had never felt more religious
than I did at that moment.

I follow up with a silent
estimate of how many more strides
we have to go before, God.
Save me.
We were more than a few
Hail Mary's away.

She uses adjectives like
dirty & stupid
as spearheads
to kill any temptations
I had of being promiscuous
let alone sexually active
as a teen.
I was too young to have children
referring to me as Our Father.

All I kept thinking about
was getting extra dibs
on the blood of Christ.

As if I hadn't felt crucified enough,
she crosses me,

"Sometimes I just hope,
that when you get that feeling
you know it is ok to go into the bathroom and..."

Holy Shit.
Holy Shit.
Holy Shit.

I stop her before
anymore talk of sin
embarrasses Jesus.
In my world,
Mary and mom are miracles,
giving birth by way of immaculate conception.
I refused to allow facts
to sway my belief, I was prepared to be
a fundamentalist.

A few feet from divinity's temple
and blessed water,
she lets me know the most important thing
I am to understand, are her intentions.

"I'd rather be having this conversation and going to church
with you,
rather than without."

Guardian Angel - 1
Dirty Panty Girls – 0

Bonafide Rojas

BORN TO RUN

there are nights we learn to run so fast
that our shadows can't keep up
we learn to blend in dust when flashing lights call our name
we grow up on trains, typical city kids in new york
learning to love the bright lights that remind us of god

we learn to blend in dust when flashing lights call our name
we want to be concrete like the streets,
stand so tall that everyone can see us.
learning to love the bright lights that remind us of god
because we are the faithless few that only depend only on ourselves

we want to be concrete like the streets,
stand so tall that everyone can see us
for tomorrow is nowhere while we're awake
because we are the faithless few that only depend only on ourselves
together we live with madness as a counterpart

for tomorrow is nowhere while we're awake
holding on to our sacred code of brotherhood
together we live with madness as a counterpart
with the whole world on our backs

holding on to our sacred code of brotherhood
we sleep under the watchful eye of the moon
with the whole world on our backs
we were born to run like the wind that we are

we sleep under the watchful eye of the moon
we grow up on trains, typical city kids in new york
we were born to run like the wind that we are
there are nights we learn to run so fast
that our shadows can't keep up

GRAND CONCOURSE SOLITUDE

if my eyes cry
black laced red concrete poetry
i would paint the concourse bright blue

weep with solitude
in schools and sideshows
sing when wounded angels
walk the streets misplaced and disheveled

my pale skin filled with coal
and swallowed ribbons to kiss death
dressed in white

when you fly with little wings past tremont
laugh like a hurricane
hear what happens
these shaking teeth, jaw and feet explode
by echo park

i could die for how sweet you are
in these rivers of crimson you rise out of

i live with broken gods
sick soldiers and rotten crowns
i would die to see you with sunken eyes forlorn

on Mt. Eden
i gather smoke and oblivion
with a funnel biting the fire
to grow vines for your bones
revealing everything to the shadows

the smells of sweet roses sing raucously
i glimpse at your lips
pale mouth of saliva

if i could fill a hall
with sobbing corpses and metallic cries
it would be to see
your broken smile

your dying clothes
your sad euphoria
your ballads of the doom
your fingerprints of blood
your dress covered with ashes
your mask dragging your love
your veins are singing

let me pierce you with dull knives
come with me where solitude is king
among these roses of swords and pins
stand where Poe once stood
where wind from the west
slips into your mouth

let me wear you like black lightning
young and pure

when there is no one left
let us speak simple

what are we if not servants of many and masters of few?
these bitter daggers find our ribs

where is the beating heart of man?
is he ready to die?
there are no protests
these bodies flow within an endless river
these altars have been worn away by the flood

see the world
the streets
the salt
the smoke
the wounds
the blindness
the anger
the disheartening
the wretched
the thorns
the sins
there is nothing left but the stones

here
you have many things that can offer you nothing
and that's when you realize
that solitude will slowly
get you to put back on your rotten crown
will that be your downfall?

THE ENTANGLEMENT

let me be your secret
your whisper
your midnight moment

let my scent stay with you all night
my voice
my morning glory

let my skin stay under your nails
my saliva
my lion's mane

let me stare at you
and watch my pupils expand
watch my hand grab your leg close

look around
remember what's here
books, shirts, vests, the letter B, guitars

let us watch the moon
as she watches us
slow dance to George Harrison

this flame we carry
we hold close to our mouths

let us be tangled like knots
in our throats trying to push
our names out

CRIMSON BLOOD WITCH

when you arose like a flower
i rushed to sketch your thorned spine
because i knew it wouldn't be in the same position
after your shed the chlorophyll of your kiss

our tongues like braille, communicate silently
your mouth is an extinguished pilot light
that when i am allowed to,
ignite with a barrage of matches committing suicide for your fire
a burn from your stomach that rises up
and spews into my mouth like lava

I eat passion off your shoulders
share the wrists with no pain involved
the bite marks fade in time
which gives us reason to bite again

you are a meal I never saw coming

we share space like pillows
eat eyelashes in the morning
taste our voices on sundays
drink mangos from hands
swallow redemption at 7:am
observe skin move to voice
press callous into fingers
create noise to flood the house
paint a new mask for family
smile for caressed bones
curse dreams and their eyes
study liberating thieves
whisper for the longing
count away loneliness as your friend
watch the flickering lights
press red buttons to love
steal my name and put in your mouth
love the present as much as the beginning
let us get drunk off the hours of our love
bind me in hot bloody sugar
make my chest yearn for your teeth

discover me with your carmine kiss
and the bleeding caress of my hand

let us share ginger, which tastes like your skin
lotus positioned with a cinnamon that is only matched
by the fireflies in your ribcage

we are patient lovers
with each other insecurities and flaws,
armed with kisses,
we share stories that we carry like anchors
and boulders on a hill

we allowed our defenses down
and showed our faces swollen
with eyes drowning in the dark

i have never felt more beautiful
than the time you listened to my wounds
bandaged them with whispers & guitar strings
that i haven't taken off since

your neck smells like eucalyptus
dressed in brown silk wrapped around your waist
like a present for our collection of good nights

here on a bed we can call our own
we lose our names in between the sheets
i found my initials on the floor
next to the stacks of books that need to be read

the lights are dim; the music is playing
there are two apples waiting for us

i take your breath from guava & chocolate
place love in my hand and use it to color the world

your hair is tangled in my throat
but i have no fear of being choked

love is a moment that i carry like markers

writing on walls to say we exist
i will paint your name in burgundy
on white walls where we can be cardinals together
in a land of common doves
rubies in the streets of diamonds
in the white of the storm, the fervor of your skin
keeps my blood solar hot

let us heal the wounds of the night before and be grateful
for the day will understand how hard it is to love unconditionally

we will run through the wind of this city
swirling like hummingbirds

when you lay on black & white tapestries
your scarlet peeks from the side
you are edible in that dress

we are not interruptions
electric currents from finger to feet
thunderbolt kiss
blood witch has my attention
open my stomach
push your dedication in
when i say thank you
say you're welcome

be aware of my hands for
they claim shoulder blades as theirs

our feet are tangled like
decade old phone chords
stretched from there to now
in your sleep you search for
my hand and squeeze the dust off

I taught myself that even though
you are as strong as onyx
your core is also delicate like flower

our passion is terra cotta in the morning
maroon at high noon

copper at nightfall

bite my throat as it swallows your sighs
you ask me how much do i love you
and i raised my hand in excitement

In this redless town, we mark corners with our
fingerprints to show ourselves we've been here

we try to change their ideas of what we are
that we are built on the thought of
love and passion, not lies and lust

we show them our palms- they're glowing feverishly
we'll smile because we know why and we'll never tell anyone

the rain is washing away the winter of yesterday
& preparing us for the spring of tomorrow

we sit in darkness because in darkness
we reinvent ourselves in the image of love

listen to the streets full of water
listen to the rain run on the concrete
singing your name in devotion

the world only sees the frame
but not the picture, the beauty,

they don't see the color of your love
as it radiates off your skin
a beautiful shade of crimson

Luzma Umpierre

ON WEAVING
For Nemir

Weaver of dreams
today you gift me your scarf
of turquoise threads of your mother's blue,
 lost in her knitting, her dream.

Island weaver,
the tenderness of the knit
pierces my thinning life
abrasing with needles
my entrails in your interfold.

Weaver of metaphors,
turquoises that blaze
you loop the small inroads of emptiness
in my alma and
in your intertwine,
I see a quietude
a mother in repose,
an infant girl afloat
from her womb--
her soul,
a shredded mesh.
Spin, my weaver, your pain
construct your own abode,
compose all of your laments
into a braid
and gift it to the waters back home.
Weaver of poems, my weaver,
Your mantle is our island of hope.

THE ENCOUNTER

Cambridge in winter
and I have driven south
from the empty pines of Maine
seeking a greener green
than the yerbas at home
on an island
to satisfy this optical nerve of mine,
disfigured by age, that now lives
in equatorial blindness.

Cambridge in dead of winter
and you are flying in a wrongful
migrant path–South to North–
like an ave enloquecida
seeking for a homeward womb
to console the solitude of your alma.

It is destined--
the threads of my mother's handkerchiefs
and your mothers knitting
reach a crescendo in their Heavenly sewing
that brings a crisscross to our lives
and a puzzle to an end
under warmer March skies
in a city known for its cries of freedom.

You touch down and I ascend,
both on frenzy for words.
Cambridge is not our island
but the Charles looks out our window
as a reminder of el Río Grande de Julia.
And we submerge into each other's body,
a ripple rises
fermented by years of waiting
and aging
but savored by the salt sent to us by an ocean
pouncing down
from our thighs and into each other's empty crevices.
We reach high tide at noon.
Like mammal whales, you call us,

mating in a dance of passion
where we both become the music and the lyrics
of our own lament.
Apasionada de ti, you whisper;
Manchada por ti, I respond.
Words that suffice
to fill our years of quiet apostolate
seeking our homeland
in extranjera worlds of the flesh
not baptized by our tongues.

Cambridge in the whiteness of snows
but our selves have been recovered
in this long lasting dance and counter dance
in which we mate and bite
the fauna and the flora of an island
in our exude.

Cambridge in the dead of winter.
And I just had absinthe,
Artemisia,
my green-eyed fairy.
Nemir, in Croatian,
you are immortal-
sap that escapes from your ulva
I imbibe
bringing unending existence
in the never ending
cycle of life that is our oneness—
our only island.

TRANSCENDENCE
for Ethel Sager

He regresado a la ciudad
a soltar a Julia
en mis adentros,
a dormir en la acera este diciembre,
a congelarme los glóbulos de sangre
que salen de mi sexo,
a golpear mis pies
en las parrillas del subway,
a despeinarme, a desgreñarme
el pelo de acá arriba y
el de allá abajo.

He vuelto a la ciudad,
a llenarme los zapatos de espuma,
a rozar mis tetas contra
los cuerpos de la gente en las calles,
a que me toquen las nalgas,
a rezar con aquel hombre
perturbado que me compra una taza de té,
a ver al pueblo hablar de mí en las calles,
a observar, a imaginar, que el mundo se viste
de azul eléctrico o rosa chocante.

He entrado en la ciudad
a abandonar la ropa,
a vestirme de primavera en el invierno,
a declararme prisionera política,
a no bañarme,
a olvidar dónde he dejado mi coche,
a ser conducida por la policía.

Algunos querrían ponerme
al cuello una cadena y pasearme
como a una perra callejera.
Otros querrían llamarme
una mujer loca.
Todo por Margarita,
siempre por Margarita,
para poder besar,

uno a uno,
los labios de su amarillo sexo.

NO HATCHET JOB
for Marge Piercy

They would like
to put the tick and flea collar
around her neck and
take her for walks on sunny afternoons
in order to say to the neighbors:
"We have domesticated this unruly woman."

They would like
to see her curled up on the corner,
fetal position, hungry, un-nursed
so that they can enter the scene,
rock-a-bye her to health
to advertise in the Woman News or Psychology Today:
 "We have saved; we have cured this vulnerable woman."

They would like
to see her unclean,
10 days without showers,
in filth and foul urine,
frizzled hair and all,
her business in ruins,
her reputation in shambles,
her body repeatedly raped on a billiard board
so that they can say in their minds:
"We have finally reduced this superior woman."

They would like
to have her OD on the carpet,
anorexic, bulimic and stiff on her bed
so that they can collect a percentage for burial
from the deadly mortician:
"We have found you this cadaverous woman."

They would like
to spread her ashes at sea,
arrange pompas fúnebres,
dedicate a wing or a statue in her name
so that their consciences
can finally rest in saying:

"We have glorified this poet woman."

But headstrong she is unleashed,
intractable she nourishes her mind,
defiantly she lives on in unity,
obstinately she refused the limelight, the pomp, and the glory.
Eternally she breathes
one line after next,
unrestrained, unshielded
   willfully
   WRITER
   WOMAN

ONLY THE HAND THAT STIRS
KNOWS WHAT'S IN THE POT

I don't
share my recipes with them-
these are folder-marked
in my brain.
Some old, from the island, you know,
some new, made in sexual passion
for the most recent of lovers,
none borrowed,
many blue.
"I need to know
the special ingredient
in this tasty dip."
"I have a prominent guest
and need your flan recipe."
One a man, the other a woman;
both wanting my gist,
my mysterious herb,
my prescription.
I don't deliver!

No handing out my set of ingredients,
they sauté in my head,
inside a Corning food dish.
I cater to friends-
eight course meals
for deliverance,
for arousing of passions,
melting aphrodisiacs for pulsating lovers.
But no partaking of formulas;
carbohydrates, fats,
proteins and supplementary substances
to sustain, to repair,
to furnish with energy;
fermentation in my gray cells,
fool's parsley from my breasts,
savory aromas from my loins,
all for the guests in my banquets.
But no handy recipes or
longevity plasmas

to take out; to go;
fast food service
offered elsewhere!

MADRE

No bebí de tu leche,
no tuve en mis labios
tus cómodos pezones,
no sentí tu amargura.

En tiempos de antaño
padecí de anorexia
por no tener tu elixir.
Más tarde con la sabiduría,
me vino el ansia de caminar
por cuerpos en busca
de tus zumos.

Deambulé buscando tu refresco
en labios que se abrían
en mi boca.
Fui chupando flores,
libando pétalos,
tragando musas
de todos los colores.
Fui trepándome
en los montes de Venus,
descendía mil cavernas
y me bajé por grutas y por grietas
de la carne.

Ciega de tu sabor,
te busqué
en la sal de las cuencas,
en los condimentos del sudor,
en la sazón de lenguas extrañas.

Toqué masas fuertes y débiles,
todas extranjeras,
según iba escalando.
Saboreé los limones,
bebí hiel,
mastiqué el hielo
en el descenso;
todo por comprenderte.

Y heme aquí hoy, madre,
intoxicada en jugos de Margarita,
feliz, al fin, de conocerte
y saborearte en este líquido rojo
que escapa por mi piel.

Paul S. Flores

ARROZ CON POLLO

Come to my house for dinner, compa
Estamos cocinando
Arroz con pollo
Tostones
Frijoles negros

We'll have antojitos
on red mantos
Mojitos to brighten
your mente with mint
Tune your ear to clave
Clap on your lap
Lightly and on time
like ajo and lime
on everything

We will greet you with the scents
warm olive oil and garlic
Roasted red and green pepper
sautéed with onion,
cumin and oregano
The aroma will primp your appetite
Make you want to pasear
Chat at the lip of a ventana
Feel the coquettish breeze
Admire palm leaves that
wave like sabanas in the wind

Ahora sí, asere
Te invito a mi casa
Plantains mashed by hand
rubbed like fingers over a cajón
We use paper
Not a tostónera
Because we like tostones thin

Black beans soaked overnight, softening
to your taste
Frijoles negros
so sweet with rum

and red wine vinegar
they even s-s-s-s-simmered in the
muanga of Orquesta Aragón

Come to my house for dinner, mi herma
Seguro que
we won't disappoint you
Tonight my señorita's cooking
arroz con pollo
estilo Cubano
so exquisite
so delicious
so perfect
Because she is the one
who makes the dish
a reflection of her soul

Golden
rice moist
but not wet
con guisantes and Spanish chorizo
Roasting, frying and baking
Ese chicken
rubbed with paprika
para que te pica
Spice in the bite
sharp and crisp

Como café
después de una siesta
Awake in the tastes and textures
Open your palette
like windows open
on humid green mountainside

Come share the table with us
Savor the cuisine
Hay ambiente
Must be a celebration
I wrote this poem
to be like an invitation
Bring your lover

and your mother
Because this is a meal
you will want to remember

FOUR FATHERS

When I was nine years old
my mother decided to marry a man
with a red beard.

Abuelo Enrique said:
"Never trust a man with a beard.
He may be hiding something.
Cortez had a beard.
And you remember
what happened to Cuauhtémoc,
don't you?"

I kept looking for signs of insincerity,
but only found my stepfather's
Viking grin, a staple of his
"Old Time" personality.
He loved Jack Daniels
and tooling around with his 1946 Roadster
more than me or my mother.

Four years later, we left the trimmed suburbs
for a two bedroom apartment,
Chef Boy-R-Dee,
and coin laundry on Sunday.
I didn't ask my mother why
we gave up financial security
and a middle class nuclear family.
But I had a feeling
some prophecies were self-fulfilling.

I'm sure my mother had found out
the ugly truth
about the bearded Viking,
but chose to let me figure out
what type of man I would be:
Whether I would choose to grow a beard
Or not.
My own father was a phantom
          A wannabe philosopher
          Who only called

when he was inspired.
He wrote dense letters
packed like cigarettes with epistemology
that burned my image of a man
into an ashtray.
He was not an Indian.
But he still couldn't grow a beard,
or a bank account to save his life.

One day your acquaintances
might only be the people who serve you drinks.
You will smell like old newspapers and damp corduroy.
And you will only be held to account
by the poetic solitude of your fatherless insecurities.

Because now you have a son.
And he wants to walk
        more like run
hallway to the door, back and forth.
        But he is not yet one.
His kneecaps are still developing.
So he falls and bangs his head on the wood floor,
        howling at the pain
and the fright of falling.

I act like nothing happened,
as if I could fool him out of his tears.
But my son is looking at me like I am a bully.
And something inside tells me he's right.

        I could be gone.
        I could disappear
        looking to find myself,
                the man I was supposed to be.
        Gone looking for God
        Gone looking out for number one
        Gone to write
                My days of solitary adventure/
                corner stacks of dog-eared books,
                a pot of cold coffee
                cigarette smoke and sandwich meat.

I could grow a beard.
Persuade myself
that this is what sacrifice
and personal freedom looks like.

But I want my son to trust the traits I carry.

I want to be present
to pick him up from his howling place.
I want him to sympathize
and understand
what dignity in the place of pride,
what responsibility in the place of attitude
what a macho really looks like.

Then I kiss his hands.
Kiss his knees.
And kiss his feet.

So he knows that men can be trusted not to leave, too.

SANTA ROSA

Leaving behind a black thread of asphalt tied to San Francisco's international orange doorknob, the poet pied piper of the Chicano hormiga supernova rolls through the northern vineyards in his '66 Chevy, bumping the new Jay Z, windows up, as the temperature outside the city limits climbs twenty-five degrees. Roll the windows down and breathe. Instead of glory he sees crosses in the peach orchards, crosses in the grape vines, crosses in the strawberry fields. Cross rows of service and rejection where martyrs became co-opted by Apple Inc. while the suburbs became the city.

He knows what he will find in Santa Rosa. The same thing he found in Pittsburg, in Modesto and Vallejo. Barrio youth that used to live in the Mission District of San Francisco forced out/back the way their parents came when they immigrated. Used to participate in the inner city summer art camp. Used to take samba, capoeira, and sugar skull classes at the cultural center. Were on their way as future artistas of la Galería de la Raza. Could have continued emblazoning murals of peace over the City's amplified homicide statistics, and increased the documentary videos of youth dignity. But now they reside in a low-income housing complex in Santa Rosa's Apple Valley.

Here the poet pied piper of the Chicano hormiga supernova will find sixteen ambivalently suspicious young raza faces ringed with orange detritus of government subsidized hot cheetos. Sixteen pre-teens, tweeners, and teenagers, plus a few adult supervisors, barely eighteen but wiser beyond their years, synthesized and edited into a municipal trailer crammed with a foosball table and broken computers, a stereo surround sound big screen TV with a Playstation connection and Wii handy, low rider and tattoo graphics pinned to the blue upholstered walls like set decoration for the laugh now, cry later tour.

This is a tiny trailer that serves as a rec center fifty miles north of the Mission, and I'm the poet trying not to show less than a professional touch. This is my first day of a residency that's supposed to last a month. It's hard to imagine how an MFA I'm still paying for got me this far. But after driving for an hour I don't have time to think how I feel a little depressed about the surroundings of my stage and audience, so I project an alter-ego everybrownman superhero character and start to bust. Not knowing how many speak Spanish or English, I trust when they hear something in either one, they'll let it be known whether they like it or not. Then mouth holes drop like dominos into laughter, confusion, boredom, and astonishment over thirty minutes of spoken Spanglish Bay Area love notes delivered in mesmerizing rhythm and flavor. They want to recite my lyrics with me. So the heavy metal and professional wrestling fans tell me, Do it again. Represent, Representa!

But my purpose isn't just a performance to watch. So we make dialogue out of it. I ask them to write about the difference between the way the world sees them and how they see themselves by comparing their identities to day and night, and then excuse myself to use the restroom. Come to find out it's a port-a-potty outside around back. The city hasn't fixed the bathrooms in the trailer for over a month, and I wonder how they had money to pay for my presentation but not repair the toilets. Needless to say the port-a-potty is shitty, smeared and wack. I can't use it. No wonder out of a project of four hundred residents only fifteen youth came to hear me rap. Outside I stare through a large hole in the chain link fence. Past the train tracks a pair of grape pickers carrying Kendall-Jackson sacks piss under a tree. But I decide not to act in accordance and wait until the second hour is up so I can drive away to relieve myself. I slowly walk back into the trailer more determined to hear what my writers came up with.

Rosie says, "By day I am a momma polar bear on the melting ice and home is further and further away. My father got stopped by ICE again on the way home from work yesterday. They would have taken his car if he'd been driving without his license. He knows never to leave home without it. But I was born in San Francisco. No one there ever stopped me or my family for being Latino. Now my dad drives a truck and we live in Rosetown. Everyone thinks we're immigrants. But we can't be deported. The boys here are rude and when I wear blue to school they call me a scrap. I used to play the clarinet at International Studies Academy, but now I can't concentrate. By day I am knocking Tupac hard in my iPod Nano. I can't take this country life shit. I went from hip-hop thugs to cowboys in rat skin boots. By night I sing the blues to my friends on MySpace. I don't study math or history. Instead I download ringtones to personalize my cell phone, and daydream about when we can move back to San Francisco. But I might have to repeat 9th grade. I'm not dumb, there's just no one to talk to."

When she reads it out loud there's a discomfort across the board, faces betraying an unfortunate feeling of guilt, or anxiety at being the next one called on to read. Not everyone comes as honest as Rosie but most see a need to express anger and frustration with their identity. Some struggle with writing in English. A few laugh it off with gangster fronts of "Oh, that's gay. Why you crying?" trying to tell me they don't care. But I know mythologizing their reality is the only way some can deal with the fact that dad is in prison and mom can't read. Is it just young people's angst, or is it a cultural creep? Before our rites of passage were junior high school crushes, sports, and weed. Now it's claiming sets, sex and ecstasy, juvenile hall and ICE raids, all before you turn thirteen. And that's when I make everyone stand in a circle to stretch their voice. First we whisper, then we scream.

On the way back to the City the dome of the SF Palace of Fine Arts preens a red terra cota monument of classic Western accomplishment. I realize there's no protection from feeling like poverty awaits you. Even though right now you may have a home there is still no guarantee someone isn't scheming to take it all away. We may not like it but they stuck us in this predicament together, citizens, and immigrants chasing the American Dream. Even though we got different issues, we take different avenues; we end up dumped in the same housing project, classroom, prison cell, parking lot, and lettuce field. The poet pied piper of the Chicano hormiga supernova is no exception. But the price of gas is going higher, and the people are being spread out further from the center. I gotta get a map of suburbia and hope that BART will soon reach Santa Rosa.

CROWBAR THING

At the height of the San Francisco Dot Com "boom," Peter Glikshtern, owner of the popular Liquid Bar on 16th Street, beat and seriously injured three Latino immigrants with a crowbar who had been drinking at his club. The event ignited feelings of violence and racism attached to the gentrification of the Mission, especially after Glikshtern was cleared of all charges.

Can I ask you a question?
Are you doing that crowbar thing?
Liquid thing, 16th Street Corridor crawl thing, that grimy thing
That thing about being hip without trying too hard,
that whole ironic thing
About telling him, telling her, telling us, telling them that we
must clean up the Mission
because cool people need a cool place to drink thing

A lookin for a good time thing, an I'm tired of the Marina thing
A Polaroid postcard crack head and prostitute thing
a hipsters in the dicey barrio thing,
an it's just like the Lower East Side thing,
graffiti on the front door, hot music and cool Dj's thing
An opportunistic—I mean optimistic thing
because can't you see the benefit
of more green space and bike lane thing
Besides how could gentrification be violent if artists started it?

Are you doing that crowbar thing?

The cash in your Oracle stock and buy a bar in the Mission thing
The protect your investment, even if it means displacement thing
The it's not personal, strictly business thing
The just trying to live the American dream thing
The white man's burden thing
The new sheriff in town thing
The show 'em your gun thing
The violence and destitution is so sexy thing
The civilize the savages thing
The vigilante thing
The cross and the crowbar thing
The Arnold Schwarzenegger thing

Are you doing that crowbar thing?

That English Only thing
That snitch to la migra when you can't stand your Latino clients
or employees thing
That drug dealers, prostitutes, and Mexicans are all the same thing
That electronic hate mail thing
That reverse racism thing
That hijole thing
That no mames, guey thing
That que tu esperabas thing
That Mexican beer is better at room temperature thing
That Glikshtern club hopping, immigrant crowbar bashing thing

Are you doing that crowbar thing?

Doing the forget about the Centro del Pueblo thing
Doing the volunteer at The Pirate Store instead thing
Doing the post-Chicano thing because I'm not political,
I'm an artist thing
Doing the more green spaces thing
because murals don't prevent violence thing
Doing the bike lane thing
because low riders aren't ecologically beneficial thing
Doing the save the whales thing
because my parents graduated from Berkeley thing
Doing the indie rock thing
because hip-hop is so misogynistic now thing
Doing that retro 80s thing
because I got bigger fish to fry so I gotta get mine thing
Doing the righteous thing because sometimes immigrants
deserve to get beat in the head with a crowbar thing

Besides, how could gentrification be violent if artists started it?

SIDEWALK LIBRARIAN

You
wanna buy some poetry?
I got Daisy Zamora,
Giaconda Bellí and Claribel Alegría
"Yo estuve mucho rato en el chorro del río."
You ever read that before?

You think I'm crazy like that dude
who stands in the doorway of the furniture store
on Valencia Street with his guitar
looking like John Cougar Mellencamp on crack
Don't you?

You are looking at my library, baby.
I will trade you a book for a burrito,
or a piece of pan dulce

The Central American poets taught me
about surviving with dignity
Do you understand me?
I ain't trying to sell poetry to nostalgic minded immigrants.
No, honey. They don't need reminding.

I got history. *Puchica.*
When I was younger this city was alive with revolution.

We started student strikes,
and held up banks to post bail
for Huey Newton and Bobby Seale.
People hijacking planes to Cuba.
We had Assata. She was the Revolution.
We had Audre Lorde. She was the Revolution.
We had Lolita Lebron. She was the Revolution.

I am a strong woman.
I am still the revolution.

What you got here now?
"Los que no tienen patria, ni nación
Sino solo una finca"

Folks with no history, no country,
just real estate.
Roque Dalton said that.

I want to walk with a bone through my hair
Teased out, and naked, except for a loincloth
Declaiming the poetry of my ancestors
with a spear in my hand
Gathering the kin together to tell the story of our migration
The wars we courageously fought, the songs we sing
the livestock we own and the tapestries we make.
I want to represent my tribe with property.
Wouldn't that be something?
If I stood out here and told the truth
... about property
Wouldn't that be real?

You wanna buy some poetry?
Everyone wants to live in a loft with big windows.
Like a big fishbowl.

Shoot, I want to live in one, too.
I want to live in one of them lofts
So all of you can watch me be rich.
Watch me go up and down the staircase
Watch what kind of furniture I lounge in
What kind of computer I have...

I got Daisy Zamora,
Giaconda Bellí and Claribel Alegría . . .

You a businessman under that goatee?
Gonna get your eyelids tattooed?
Want your private parts pierced?

Listen, honey.
I got a jaguar tattooed on my soul
My lips been pierced by a quetzal feather
dipped in America's veins
I used it to spell my name
on a check for forty acres and a mule.
The bank took my picture and Xeroxed it.

It was performance art.

Hold your wallet close round here.
Treat it like an anchor.
Otherwise you might start to believe
what I got is really worth something.
You might buy yourself a clue.

If you're an undercover type fella
we got plenty of other games to play.
Around the corner is Oliver North's cousin
He got contraband from Iran.
As a matter of fact, here
Give him one of these.
Pobrecita
Remember to tell him I sent you.

Today, it's free
And if you don't like that book
I'll give you your money back.
Guaranteed.

I got Daisy Zamora,
Giaconda Bellí and Claribel Alegría...

BROWN DREAMS

Inspired by Jorge Mariscal and Richard Rodriguez

This is a true story about a brown dream
sinking to the bottom of the Tigris Euphrates

This is a brown dream.

It was Francisco's last night out with his friends.
Three of them on their way to see the latest sci-fi movie.
They were driving.
A stereo jocking the latest top 40 rapper,
because that was all he listened to.
But it didn't matter.

Music was only part of the setting
and not the motivation for late night
brainstorms about how to make money,
or how to escape the feeling of being
left out of a dream so many painted
red white and blue.

But his dream was brown.
Brown as his skin.
Brown and impure.
Brown as Eve's apple after she took the first bite.
Brown as the everlasting blur of English, African, and Indian
moving through the forests of this continent
four hundred years ago
before it was known as destiny.
Before he had ever heard the word
"immigrant"
Beaner! Spic! Stupid! Dirty Mexican!
Before he had ever dreamt of assimilation.

He is 18 years old.
He is in San Diego,
Topeka, Buffalo, San Antonio,
Oakland, California.
He wants a piece of the American Dream.
Francisco wanted a college degree.
He wanted to be a professional,

a stockbroker, or FBI agent,
because those were the jobs with the most power.
If he could have been a rock star or a super hero
there would have been no need to enlist.
But he had to be a U.S. citizen
if he was going to make a living like them.

The Army recruiter at his high school
told him that if he served in the military
he could automatically become a U.S. citizen.
After four year's duty and an honorable discharge
there would be plenty of money left over
for him to continue his education
at a good institution.
Or he could take his technical skills
as a tank operator or small weapons expertise
and apply them to a civilian job.

It was exciting;
Brown boy who wasn't even a citizen,
who had barely been a resident five years,
who didn't know much about education,
was now willing to die to become a student.

One year later
he was working on a tank unit
fighting in Iraq.
Francisco heard it was the second time
the president had invaded this nation.
They were driving in the desert.
They were taking fire, swerving.
The tank lost control
and headed straight into the river.

As Francisco's lungs filled up with water
he remembered his last night out with his friends;
How his mother had wanted to cook dinner for him—
but he didn't want to spend another hour
in that cramped apartment
where she cooked for six of his brothers,
his two uncles and their compadres.
Instead, Francisco invited Jose and Diego

out to the movies
because that's what Americans did.

Now his soul is an ancestor in the Euphrates.
Chicano blood mixing with Arab soil,
returning to the Garden of Eden
by way of the U.S. Army,
same way it had come.

Only now, he would finally receive something
he had been promised:
An officially sealed envelope on top of Old Glory.
Citizenship had never been earned so graciously.
Even, if it comes posthumously—
Why don't they extend it to the victim's family?

The American Dream is dirty.
Why should Chicanos have to die
to earn the approval of this society?

This is a brown dream.
Brown as the bus riders union.
Brown as gasoline.
Brown as the Tigris-Euphrates
The Mississippi and the Rio Grande.
Brown as coyotes.
Brown as the blood-soaked sands of Iraq
and on the ranches of Arizona border vigilantes.
Brown as Affirmative Action in the military
but not the university.
This is a brown dream.

Roberto "Simply Rob" Vassilarakis

ROUND MIDNIGHT

'Round midnight
On the Simpson Street
Subway platform
A mother of 3
Awaits the downtown #2
Because her body is 1
Worth just a little bit more
On the stroll downtown
Than it is at Hunts Point

Hard knocks and crack rocks
Have jacked up her teeth
Ravaged her face
Buy she still has her shape

Working the streets
Has taken the place
Of sliding down poles
And private dance shows
Back in the day

Back when she wouldn't take shit
If a nigga got slick
"Boo, I'm a dancer! I ain't sucking
your dick!"
Now she gets
"$25 for brain till you're drained baby"
If she only scores one
At least she has her next hit
'Round midnight

'Round midnight
A drunk Salvadoran
Occupies his designated area
Of a basement floor
The one he shares with
7 other undocumented
Migrant workers
Cold nights even more

His attention tennis balls
Between trying to make the ceiling
Stop spinning
And a water damaged picture
Of his family

Wondering whether
Los centavos que se gana
Are worth the sacrifices made
Or if the benefits weigh
Heavier than his heart

His memory stained
With the residue
Of atrocities contained
In the light of night
And the cover of day
Stowing away
Risking his life
On north bound freight trains
Rolling toward some obscure idea
Of a promised land
Cruzando ciudades y campos
Ríos y desiertos
To work 12 hour days
Bellow minimum wage
A modern day slave
'Round midnight

'Round midnight
A dude kisses his girl
Tasting her tears
As they roll down her face
Past her lips
Collecting themselves
On his tongue
Clouds hover above her
Like white lies
Big dark shades cover her eyes
As she cries
She tries to apologize
For getting caught

Between her love and his fist

To which he replies
"I ain't never known a love like this.
I'll never leave. You're all I need."
'Round midnight

'Round midnight
A New York City Poet
Writes another draft
Of who he is
Redesigning and
Redefining himself
With every
Stroke of his pen
Laying his demons to rest
Between the lines

Write poet
Write as if your life depends on it
Write as if your world
Is bigger than the inside
Of your head
And the limits of your vision

Write as if your poetry is
The only one kept
In a world of empty promises
Like your mother never told you
Your father wasn't ever
Coming home
She didn't have to
It was already understood
Let these poems serve
As cataloged reminders
Of who and where you've been
When you've lost
And found your way
And of what
You are not

Scribe

Scribe as if your manhood
Is in question
As if the ones you've needed most
Have turned their backs
And walked away

As if you can live
Without their love
Or feel
without your mamas touch

Scribe as if you know
You're better off
As you lay naked in your bed
With only your pen and notebook
Between you
And the sheets
'Round midnight

HOMBRE BELLO

Como el mar llamándome
Cautivándome
Ojos tan profundos
Hacen que mi mundo
Se llene de ilusión

Será el una bendición
O una maldición
No se si seguir con este tema
O dar media vuelta
Irme lejos de esta situación

Hombre Bello
Has the deepest eyes
Like the hypnotic motions
Of exotic oceans
Eyes that mesmerize
They pull me in like an undertow
Like the rip tide
While my own betray me
Telling him without discretion
Everything they refuse to hide

Las palabras me las llevan el viento
No las encuentro
Como explicar mi sentimiento

Pocas
Breves
Las veces
Que lo e visto

Pasa el tiempo

Me pregunto
Esto es mutual
O sera como un cuento
Que por puro deseo me lo invento
Este amor
Que me vive por dentro

Lo habrá visitado
En cualquier momento
Aun con el mas pequeño
De sus pensamientos

Could he love a struggling man
One holding it together
With rough and calloused hands

A mans character can not be
Developed with ease
Somewhere in life I've taught
Myself to believe
That I shouldn't have regrets
But I do

Can't bring myself to ask him
I wonder
If he feels me too

I light a candle on the alter
Top a little piece of paper
Baring his name

A symbol of love

Hope is born with my request
I lay down to sleep
Placing my head to rest on hopes chest

The flame flickers as it whispers
The answers to my questions
But I can't understand what it says

If I should die before I wake
A thousand dreams
I would surrender
Just to hold him in my arms
And never let him go

HERITAGE PIECE

Hay herencia y cultura
Held in my bis abuelas veiny hands
Clapping
Mientras haciendo pupusas
De frijol y queso
Con un ritmo que mímica
El pal pito de mi corazón

I long to hear the melody
Of her native tongue
Speaking her native tongue
Echo's of an Mayan ancestry

I ache to walk
Los caminos forged by
Pies descalzaos de gente indígena
Before the first cobblestones
Were placed onto its soil

Before Spain came
In her tall ships
Bearing cannons
Landing on it's black sand beaches
To change it's language
Of Nahuat to Español
And it's name
From Cōzcatlān to El Salvador

But one man's warrior
Is another man's savage

Any way they sliced them

The blood that was spilled
Is in part the same as the one that
Floods my ventricles

Yo soy Guanaco
Envuelto como un tamal
En hojas de elote

I am el sabor de Loroco
And the fragrance of Flor Izote

With this heritage scribe
Written in the languages
Of their conquerors
I pay homage
To my fallen tribes
I honor their lives
With my fist held high
And with my warrior cry
Ahooah!

SEEKER

I knew this cat named Seeker
Who was in search of something deeper
He handled his
He wasn't a sleeper
I've met mad heads in my lifetime
Seeker was a keeper

I had his back
He had mine
We were always side by side
I remember when I knew him
He was living two lives

In one he was a rainbow
That stretched across the sky
Made up of sunlight
Through the raindrops
Shining the colors of his pride

In the other he had to hide
Keeping the truth inside
While longing for the day
He didn't have to live a lie

We were eighteen
He was the eldest of five
Being the man of the house meant
That his youth and education
Fell by the waste side compromised
BUT
Seeker was street
And otherwise wise
You see he taught himself to read
By sounding out the street signs
The way he read street signs
To himself in his mind

His motto was
"Only the strong survive. Only the strong survive."
Sometimes he'd say it

As he'd mush me
Then he'd look at me and smile

He said it on that one day
That one day was a Sunday
That Sunday was Gay Pride Day
Gay Pride Day in the sun day
Having fun day
Gettin' some day
It was you don't have to hide day
Take your shirt off
Show your pride day
Wave your rainbow colored flag day
Not five kids one crib day
But scan for ass at the parade day
Makin out with other dudes day
The cameras panning through the crowd day
The Sunday Evening News played
His mother saw him on TV
And now she knew that he was gay
I couldn't offer him a place to stay

When he got home he was disowned
The man of the house was now dethroned
The last thing he EVER heard his mother say was
"No quiero hijo maricon!"

I knew this cat named Seeker
Who was in search of something deeper
But what he found was
Something like a phenomenon
Something that keeps going on and on

I'm talking about kids
Selling their bodies on the streets
They live on
The other things he found were
His stomach empty
And a park bench to sleep on
Giving the popo someone to peep on
Creep toward
Then leap on

In order to wake him up with the jolt
Of a night stick

Sometimes he might hook up with a trick
Who'd pay him a few dollars
To lick his balls and suck his dick
One night he scored an over-nighter with a stranger
And the thought of a warm shower
And a soft bed to sleep on
Made him blind to the signs
Of impending danger
So he agreed willingly
For a one hundred dollar fee

His body was discovered the next morning
Beneath ominous storm clouds that were forming
When I got the call from the detective
It was already storming
He asked me if I knew him
I wasn't sure just what to say
Because he called him by his government name
And I never heard him referred to that way

I said I couldn't help him
I didn't know that name
But he gave me a number to call anyway
As soon as I hung up
I threw that shit away
And started to get ready
Because I had plans with my man Seeker
Later that same day

When I left my crib
I saw a rainbow in the sky
So I fell to my knees on the wet sidewalk and started to cry
Because I knew that very instant
It was Seeker saying goodbye
"Only the strong survive. Only the strong survive."
But one of them had died
I guess he no longer seeks the day
He doesn't have to live
A lie
A lie
A lie

Caridad de la Luz "La Bruja"

WTC

World Trade Center
What's the Cause?
Work to Change
Wish to Connect
Want to Cry
Watched them Climb
Watched Towers Crash
Wishes Turned Cloudy
Whispered to Christ
Watch the Children
Wish Time Could
Wash this Clean
Witness the Corruption
War that Conquers
W Targets Countries
White Torn Cloth
Wrists Turned Cold
Watched the Cloud
Wrap the City
Watched the Calamity
Work towards Charity
Women Try Calming
Weakness to Courage
Worthless to Cooperate
Watching Them Corroborate
Wounds to Clean
Working to Counterbalance
Winding the Clock
Willingness to Counsel
Wife Tries Cooking
Washing the Clothing
Working the Corner
Writing to Courts
Well-wishing the Children
Wanting to Create
Worlds to Cradle
Want to Cover
Wrong to Cry
Wisdom Takes Crossroads
Warriors Think Consciously

Waiting to Contact
Witches Turned Counselors
WTC

LETTER TO MY SON

Haiku-
I have written a
letter to the man my son
will one day become

You are not a child anymore, though you were a beautiful boy, a man is what you are now, maybe almost a man.

You can call yourself a man once you have mastered how to hammer a nail into wood and create a home, when you can love a woman enough to understand that which you dislike or fear about her. If you have made the love that births a child and stayed each day to raise it, you can also raise your head high and call yourself a man.

Challenges are not obstacles, they are steppingstones, and if you have never set foot upon one to see the next level, you are not a man. If you've stopped climbing after the first steep step, you are only half a man. If you have learned to dance wildly enough to make thunder crash at your feet, you are not a man but a God!

You are a God if the lightning you create has been harnessed to illuminate the darkest paths. You are a man if you have stumbled through the darkness without knowing how to make fire. You are a man if you can see the fire in a woman and find warmth there. You are a God if you shelter her flame from the rain without letting her burn you. You are not a man if you have pummeled her flame to mere cinders and let your tribe grow cold in winter.

You are not a man if you have procreated and ran so far that you did not teach the child to stand, did not cradle its hand, and did not try to understand the questions in its eyes. If you've hunted for food, fed the world knowledge, and kept a well clean for others to drink, you can call yourself a savior.

If you ate only what was given, explored the corners of a box you live in, knew well what was wrong and right but kept sinning or remained indifferent, then you are a slave. If you have spread your wings and tasted the future but still landed in the past, then you are an ass.
If you have read this letter with passion and hunger, looked for the message inside yourself, loved the mystery, cried from misery, and still was able to smile, then you are not a man, a God, a savior or a slave but you truly are my Son.

MATADOR

I was born wild, with strong thick muscles stacked to stampede,
Bred with pedigree to chase dreams of conquest,
defiance, victory, and alliance
Bully by nature, a force misunderstood, mistreated and abused. Territorial
and aware, too proud to show fear, tested by the masses and consumed by the
hands that force-feed for selfishness and greed
Thrown into arenas to be watched by ravenous eyes, loved,
and despised at the very same time
The death dance you lure me into, with spectators abound, cheering the sight
of our duel, hungry for blood, thirsty for the ghastly scene and crying for the
cruel-ended tradition.
How I reveled in my ambition to forge my way free,
ready to destroy all that stood before me.
While you, Matador, adorned from head to toe with a snarling smile like the
crescent moon, posture of a crane.
You have a tongue for a sword, hidden gracefully behind the red cape of your
lips, luring me with the seaward sway of your hips.
Whom would I convince not to challenge me this way
if not you, Matador?
After inviting me to come, you challenge me to run,
tease me to chase, trick me to die.
We rhythmically gamble eye to eye,
I can almost taste your desire to pound my hide.
You knew that in the face of this I would thrust forward powerfully, horns first,
ready to gore your taunting stance,
willing to take on each painful lance
How graceful you are with your bolero-covered chest,
gold-buttoned breast
The beautiful killer of my natural whim, how swiftly you glide with silken
stockings over your shins.
Lucky are you to win
but maybe today the dance will end
and the tip of my horn will wear you thin.

SPIC

Speak Politely I'm Crazy
Start Participating In Culture
Speaking Purposefully Is Constitutional
Socio Political Insanity Continues
Speaking Powerfully Involves Commitment
Spain Probably Isn't Caring
Statehood Probably Isn't Coming
Society prefers indifference collectively
Strong Pro-Independence Community
Separated People Inevitably Crumble
Spanish People in Crisis
So Petty it's Crazy
Similar Patterns in Chimps
Solidarity Provides Immediate Connection
Sharing Perspective Is Cleansing
Shutting Pie-holes Isn't Cool
Seize P-Ricans in Chancletas
Spiritualists Praying Ignite Candles
Some Poetry Is Censored
Speak Properly In Code
Stupid People Inspire Comedy
Some Propaganda Isn't Criticized
Super Powers Inherited Culturally
Stop Praising Ignorant Celebrities
Slander Purposely Impairs Confidence
Surviving Peoples Insensitive Comments
Spic Poetry Isn't Criminal
Seeing Persecution Is Crushing
Still Placed In Cadenas
Selling Poison in Clinics
Still Pondering Island Connection
Solar Power Is Clean
Spending Plenty in Cash
Spaniards Pummeled Indigenous Caciques
Stop Parades Including Columbus
Slavery Practiced In Caribbean
Scarred Permanently Inventing Cures
Shoe Points Impale Cockroaches
Stepping Past Indignant Critics
Staying Poised Inside Conflict

Soy Perfecta Inventando Caridades
Solo Puedo Imaginar Calma
Sexy Pero Inteligente Coño

EL BOTELLÓN

Había una vieja
Con piel de canela
Buscando agua
Para cocinar su
Miel de abeja
Curandera
Con remedios que
Le enseño la abuela
Para mandar lo malo
Afuera P' Afuera – Fuera
Con su fuego
Y candela
Limpiando toda la tierra
Con Agua y leña
Lo que practica
Nos enseña
Salvando la selva
Y los ríos de pureza
Después de esta siesta
Empezamos la fiesta
Celebrando la vieja buena
Que guarda fronteras
Ayudando
Familias entera
Ella nos empreña
El alma lo llena
Aliviando las penas
Con magia

Que se encuentra en su Botella

Emanuel Xavier

CONQUEST

Your absence is the pillow used to cuddle at night, with you next to me, as the
moon watches over the despair of this darkness.

Distant and cold like the snow of mountains.
It is my cue to leave in the morning.

This rose, my heart, will not have sunlight to bloom here.
Tears will not provide enough rain to sustain this life.

Your demons revel in their fire.
Your songs lure another shipwrecked soul.

Your beauty disguises your myths, like religion.
Wars waged without necessity, out of fear.

What brought us to the tomb of this bed was only meant to be a dramatic kiss,
hope between wounded soldiers on a stage.

I should have tasted the blood on your lips,
caught a glimpse of a deadbeat father in your eyes.

You shot with fair warning, celebrated your victory,
heroic in your justice of killing the child with stolen toy in hand.

I will not be meaningful enough to haunt you
beyond words and I will be forgotten.

It was not your duty to hold me in your arms
without holding back and, for this, I grant you atonement.

Like the morning sun, dreams were awakened by your light
and quickly faded as reality set back in.

There was loneliness and sadness, and you were the hope.
There was violence and pain, and you were the healing.

Others will undoubtedly drown in the sea of your emotions,
get lost in your conflicts; continue to be music for the masses.

Our time shared crossing this path was insignificant- when you get to greener pastures, enjoy the air, breeze against your skin.

I will perhaps be a story maybe worth sharing, nothing more.

MADRE AMÉRICA

If I were to give myself to you completely,
would it matter that I didn't come from your womb?
I have been thrown out of homes and abandoned by fathers
looking for a place to settle and offer what little is left of this spirit.
I speak your tongue and share the beds of your sons.
I would fight in your battles if considered man enough for you
The dead eyes of innocent faces would not haunt this empty soul
Would you be my motherland?
Would I be allowed to bathe in your oceans
without drowning in your oil spills
or washing ashore a lighter skinned slave in plastic chains?
Would you hold me when I die and grant me a final resting place?
Madre, put down that newspaper and look at me closely,
I much resemble your first kin before you were raped
I have tasted your tears and washed myself in your sorrow
Madre, would you grant me sanctuary for my sin of living?
Of loving?
Your children do not want me to be part of your history.
Your daughters do not care to heal these wounds.
Madre, remind them that I have kept you strong
I have cleansed you, fed you, kept you warm.
You made me who I am today but still, unworthy of their affection.
You were always full of love for all of us.
You raised us the same even when we took your splendor for granted.
We may not have the same blood but we are all connected.
I don't want to lose this family.
This heart belongs to you.
America, you have been my mother and my father.
The autumn leaves are falling and it is only summer.
Do not let them keep me from coming into your arms.
Do not let them imprison me with lies.
Do not let them kill me for wanting to share in your devotion.
Remind them that our differences
is what makes this home more beautiful than any other.
I am nourished and wise because of you.
I look out the window and am not afraid of the wilderness outside.
I only fear not finding my way back.
Madre, I want to stay here with the others to protect you.
I want to read your musings and hear your stories.
I want to stare out at your skies at night and lay on your lands.

Madre, I know it is not you but they that are jealous of our bond.
Madre, educate us all to understand more than one language.
I want to write poetry to someday teach in your schools
Peace belongs to all of us because of you, *madre*
America, I will always be your child.

MI CORAZÓN

I search for my soul in paintbrush strokes
listen for my muse in Mr. Softee ice cream truck jingles
smile at strangers on the subway for simple humanity
This heart seems a novelty but it continues to love

It makes children out of full-grown men
withdraws the instinctive awareness of animals
It beats enough passion to arouse poetry
etching words that mean nothing yet everything

Like drums and like songs
with the conviction of dance
Like rhythm flowing from bodies
It continues to love

It has outlived history like a vampire
blood healed and stronger with time
Beauty resounding from within
Bathed in tears and sheltered from the bruises outside

City noises drown the thumping sounds
Threatened to be frozen by bitter cold
but it beats to the tune of glimmering eyes
as it unfolds to render a lonesome petal

Concrete may not supply cushion
Perverse lights may weaken the stars it craves
Hatred may wage war and hindrance
but it continues to love

It reveals itself through a kiss
The same which often hides it
Often remembered and rather forgotten
like skyscrapers offering great views but obstructing the sky

An abandoned pier surrounded by polluted rivers
It continues to love
Walls torn down for a better view of the other side
It continues to love
Projects housing poverty and lifeless dreams

elevators hauling empty designer pockets
gateways to famine and drought
It continues to love

Into nights brightened by moon
It continues to love

Life as offered by family and friends
It is the salvation and prayer for forgiveness
It continues to love

It continues
to love

THE GIFT OF RAIN

"There came a time when the risk to remain tight in the bud was more painful than the risk it took to blossom." - Anaïs Nin

The only thing queer is inhibition
Pride is the magnificent wig worn by the man who gambles living
to bring happiness to others or simply to herself
It is the freedom to explore limits and not living in fear of love

We believe like no other that we are cherished completely
No church, man, or woman could ever make us think
God or a higher being is not walking amongst us
with the colors of the rainbow

We are music, dance, poetry, art
We capture the splendor of the world around us with photography
We raise our families to believe in true equality
We pray for forgiveness, not for ourselves, but for hate-
Wings are useless in darkness

In war, men are praised for killing others
In love, we are not welcome to battle
Some are more afraid of us than torture or death
Holding guns is tolerable but not holding hands
Our rights are of more concern than poverty

This journey is with each other not with children, goats, or horses
True love does not solely belong between a man and a woman
Just like great sex does not simply belong
between two men or two women
All should be admired only for humanity and condemned for lack of

This struggle is not straight girls kissing one another
for the attention of cameras or boys
It is denial or staying silent while those around you assault your soul
If it is crazy to want to share our lives with someone special,
let it be known we are all insane

If the Lord is indeed our shepherd,
let us not kill and hang him up on fences
Quoting books that suggest women always be submissive

and never wear gold or pearls
that men never shave
or wear clothes of more than one fabric seems questionable
when our youth are forced to deal with prejudice
without the support of families
that would stand by them if faced with the same discrimination
for being any other minority

Remove everything gay from culture
and there would pretty much be nothing left

Enjoy the rainfall,
for all the ruin it seems to bring,
it also supplies us with life

MISSING

I apologize to you now
for holding back what you should know
but there are too many expectations of me
that are my own fault for sharing my life in such detail.
I have never been good at keeping things to myself
publicly sharing what most would deem personal
but I'm learning to build walls again.

Those that actually read my words look between the lines,
"Is this what he is really like?" Perhaps.
One day, you will find me again at the amusement park
I will be the little boy with the red balloon,
a runaway who found himself,
a life fulfilled prepared for death.

It was never your responsibility to save me
Others didn't recognize me from milk cartons either.
You might think I am giving you the stink eye
When, in fact, I will no longer be just half deaf but fully blind.
I will be gone as soon as you look away.

When you spot the balloon in the sky
You will realize that it wasn't a dream.
The brightness of the sun will not wash away the red.
Someday you'll see me yet again, when the time is right,
Make sure to point me out to your friends
at the amusement park, the little half deaf blind boy
with the red balloon in front of the graffitied wall.

Nancy Mercado

THE DEAD

Where I lay the dream of
following myself in your soul
        —Julia De Burgos

I face the universe
When I speak to the dead
I lay as they do
In their coffins
My body upright
Revealed to the wide expanse
Of the firmament

There I speak with mother
In some brightly-lit hallway

She says she is going
To sleep with father
His voice resonating from inside
A black room she enters

I often speak to the dead
They share their days with me
Provide advice
They have no wings
No halos
No emitting light from within
They're people just like you and like me

IN MY PERFECT PUERTO RICO

My gray mother would be
Combing her mother's white hair
On their turquoise painted porch
Under mango trees
Among hummingbirds

My black grandfather
In the next rocking chair
Happily looking on

My four-foot-eight cousin Sonia
Would be out back
In a wooden shack
Washing clothes
Or running in the garden
Tending to her dogs
She wouldn't walk with a limp
Wouldn't be sick
She'd have working kidneys
She'd live past thirty

My father would be hunting
All over this side of the island
With his best friend Angel Rodriguez
For reusable items
Dumped on the lush country side
They would be recycling pioneers

I would have a choice
Of which cousin to visit
We would still be young
And beautiful
Yolanda
Lili
Wanda
Evelyn
Ivelise
Hilly
We would still be together
And not just old scattered pieces
Of what we once were

EL COTO LAUREL

Dinner with mom
And with *tía* Carmín
Consists of a heavy soup
We call *Sancocho*
It consists of stories
About the exquisiteness
Of grandmother's cooking
How she stretched a sliver of onion
And little garlic cloves
During the Second World War
Enough to cook a pot
Of beans for two nights
How the taste of those beans
Could never be duplicated

Dinner with mom
And with *tía* Carmín
Consists of a warm sunset
White curtains flowing
In the kitchen
Annoying mosquitoes
Under the table
And highball glasses
Filled with passion juice

MILLA
-Mi Abuela, Puerto Rico

Milla lived eons ago
When sandals pounded dirt roads
Blazing hot under palm tree lined skies.
Milla's long dark hair flowed side to side,
Glistened in the noon light.
Mahogany skinned, she shopped
Plátanos, yucas, a bark of soap.
Milla worked,
Striking clothes against wooden boards,
Gathering wood for evening meals,
Feeding chickens, hogs, dogs,
And roosters at dawn.
Milla traveled only once
To Chicago,
A color-faded photograph serves as document.
Smiles and thousands of hugs
For the grandchildren on a park bench.
Milla's a century old
And still remembers every one of us
Even those left over in the U.S.
She still carries a stick
Certain of her authority
Over four generations.
Milla outlived two world wars,
Saw the first television,
The first electric bulb in her town,
Hitler, segregation,
The Vietnam War,
And Gorbachev.
Milla can speak of
The turn of the century land reforms,
Of the blinded enthusiasm
For a man called Marin
And the mass migration of the 1950's.
Milla can speak of her beloved husband,
Sugar cane cutter for life.
She can speak of the love of a people,
Of the pain of separation.
Milla can speak of the Caribbean Ocean,

The history of the sun and sand
And the mystery of the stars.
Milla maintains an eternal candle lit
Just for me.
Milla will live for all time.

ON MY RETURN FROM PUERTO RICO TO THE U.S.
OR (THE IDLENESS OF IT ALL)

It's yesterday wasting away behind our backs
Ducking at our every twist
Imploring us to return
From this cold casket where time flies robbing youth,
An alienating stare,
A decrepit course of a life time
Shown through the eyes
Of a middle-aged black woman,
Through a young Puerto Rican man
Riding the subway arguing with some imaginary figure,
An ice box shuttling people nowhere for years
Sending them off to their graves before time,
Icicle days fooling us,
Mesmerizing even the keenest of minds
Into believing time does not run out.
Rows and rows of steel and concrete,
Chemical plants and train tracks
Laughing at our misplaced sense of life,
A shivering view of barren trees
And soot-wrenched grass, defying all odds,
Standing there, daring man,
A bad joke leaving us here
In knee-deep oil slicks
With barb wire memories of childhood ignorance
Joys of family life almost forgotten.
We're misplaced in this lifeless machine
Trying to construct homes out of straw pieces in the snow,
Speaking foreign languages to those
Who run off on their way to work
To contribute to valleys that lay in waste,
We're dangling from a noose
Between epochs and conversations never begun
And, dressing up wrong,
And using chopped up words: manufactured phrases
Invented to describe a manufactured life,
We're the living dead
Idly speaking, mindlessly racing through our existence,
Aimlessly hurrying from one stage to the next
Like volunteer slaves onto the auction block

Donating to their own demise,
Supporting toxic dumps and empty faces
Combing playground sides
In search of future O.d'ed addicts,
Withering away in housing projects:
    neighborhoods used as toilets for the rich.
It's MTV across America!
Delusions of stardom!
As you side step all those crack vials past your doorway
Your mother, suffocating on a baseball field, a landfill
Approved for little league games
Where your little brothers play
All their days away,
A cold solitude, mute and still
Like everything beyond that sheet of ice covering your window,
A bird's petrified song in the wind,
A frozen tear stopped in its tracks.
Its haunting memories of an era abandoned:
    the dazzling sun on mother's tiled-kitchen floor
Adding the final touch to our afternoon meal,
Father's laughter just beyond a caress,
Mother's last kiss,
My nephew's bewildered glance,
Will I return again—

NO NOTHIN
-for Amiri & Amina Baraka

No frontin
Just fast rap,
As bop rises
Base Head's buggin,
J's feelin up girls,
While props get you
5 dead beats
In your mama's crib.

No forever love affair
But minnie made honies
Dancin reggae against
Tiny manhood's.
Stacked, mad bitches
Grinnin for starlit stories,
Chillin in Jams,
Dancin in fat gear,
While Rodney King's burnt.
2 4 me
2 4 you.

No time takin talk
Just two homies hangin hard
While Betty beat her 12 year old kid
Into the ground
Cause he wanna chill in front of their building,
Some swirm infested
Section 8 shit crib
Where fiends play.

No extended educational environments,
But nasty government criminals,
Suppliers of rat poison
For city streets
For little joey and miky and little kiki to take.
Efficient officials offering
Living hell on earth
In candy rappers.

No community get-along
But lame brains
Looking for fame
In all the wrong places.
Back-stabbing dummies,
Compliment experts,
Yes men inching their way
Toward the hype
Where media maniacs maintain the panic,
Money neutralizes nations
Under spot lit lies.

No correct history to rap about
Just losers lost in TV land
Rushin to be trippin.
Bullshitters sellin us up the creek
While youngsters gang bang,
Get capped,
Die on city streets
In the middle of " 9 0 2 1 0 "
As the man with the master plan
Keeps on side steppin
Over our bodies.

LITANY FOR CHANGE

Change the Pacific Ocean trash gyre
A swirling mass of pestilence vomiting plastic demons
Devouring the innocents of the sea

Change the melting mountains of ice
The thinning rug beneath the Polar Bears' feet
Change their early eclipse from the world

Change the wars in the Middle East
Wiping-out the children in the streets
Dressed in grey rags playing with dirt and sticks and with pebbles

Change the insatiable hunger of the rich
For diamonds and dollar bills and oil to eat and to drink
Their self indulging time bomb for us all

Change the extinction of the bats and the bees
The little hard working creatures
Who never asked us for anything in life
Change their downfall from this planet

Change our lust for ignorance and for more and more things
Our hypnotic affair with guns and ammunitions
With violence on the air and violence in our dreams

Change the foolhardiness with which we treat the earth
The yanking out of forests by the acres
Without knowing the lives there with no care for the souls there

Change our narcissism over miniscule acts of how far we've come
Our bizarre decrees of dominion over earth and sky and seas

Change the minds and the hearts of men
Their rotted countryside and blackened water ways
Their tainted winds and distempered cities

Let them be filled with color again with youth and vibrant again
Let them be lucid and living and loving again

Urayoán Noel

FORAY

(Crown Donut, 161ˢᵗ Street, the Bronx)

AAAA syncopated playing in the park   down by the apartment with the drawn curtains   where immigrants are born and die   solos in the twilight ether   sounds askew the neighbors downbeat   the orle the garland   synapse and starlight   the perfect score to the street lit teleplay   stowed in garbage trucks   the all-nite donut countertop spot check   pass the mic and live thru the murder within   side winding the bum note   how's everything?   security no homeland   never better why?   reality check cashing   cash only realty   dead in the city   they wouldn't have made it   families in freefall   shy boys like tombstones   in fluorescent diner   somersault I / quotidian We   no nation in pronomination   assertoric flow / flaw   adult diapers on cable   he who has E.D. needs G.E.D. needs G's is spotted trained to kill the impulse within   to overload the shopping cart   to flood the express line with price check items   voided coupons   as afternoon gives in to cruising eyes *AAAA* "Love to Love You Baby"   fun while you wait to decompose daily on premises   the face in the mirror   stage dive creosote babies   bound by the variable rate of deception   I speak of the self and its limits its mullet phase   its postindustrial complex   unserviceable sector   invisibility TV now comes with wireless   with no comes a where to multidimensional mass movement unmapped   could never be captured in tekne   the hackneyed delivery   the wack flow   still blows away the week-kneed audience   incipience of / and / as community   the only kind   the rest is special interest focus group granola   subprime midnite madness at the drive-in pixilation fest   nomad daemons emailaise   whatever its foibles I tell you the city still swings / seems / fumes   the high-rise imposes   the diner odorizes diasporan flaneurs   the 80s freestyle still oozes from over lit clothing stores   "Forget Me Nots" still plays at least four times per day on the dance station   as does "Le Freak" *AAAA* communities of saturation   iteration stops not later on Saturday   the store-bought beauty of want and dream   and busted hustle and bus stop breakups angry-assed repentant or simply pent   and who killed the republic? say the bells whose public?   sad futuric bells   fidget with the grim / the grime / the word whose sad chapel?   tolls for us its cavernous enormity   enough of intimacy I'm into my city shared   pensive expansive   we're still here   all of us citizens of din   denizens of now   many-festooned
destiny in songs   always about to forgo

BEACHED WAIL
2002/2009 Coney Island/Brighton Beach

No discontent this summer--
The crowds descend from trains--
Sand flies buzz the skyline-- in sequence:
Senior-citizens-turned-amateur-hedge-funders,
Professional hedge trimmers, stoner-loner-types--
Always the throng (no thongs, just lapsed non-swimmers,
Arms flailing in vain) -- all here piling their pain
onto beach blankets and flinging it to the tides

There goes the hip-hop civitas in flip-flops
There go the brokers and the breakers
There go the bathers doused with camphor
There go the last sun-bludgeoned corpses

A song has something to do with 1) the sharing
Of ordinary information 2) sunny faces and/or
Shady transactions 3) beer and/or dominoes
And/or 4) wet rooftop kisses in a sea
Of loose skin and lotion sandwiches

There go the middle-age burnout surfers
There goes the junk in too-tight jeans
There go the spliffed karaoke posses
There go the loosies and the 40s

Two six-packs later (of root beer,
That is) on the boardwalk hiccupping--
Using his best lines but not yet
Pick upping-- fate starts to sink in:
Here's to another bored walker
Humming ersatz soul
Watching crowds capsize
Into rusty beach chairs

There go the last grease fire fumes
Emptying out windowless rooms
There go the accents and the love-bites
There go the frequenters of uptown trains
And the frequenters of train wreck sites
There go the holiday revelers
There go the sandcastle levelers
There go the block demolishers
The brain demolishers, the tides
And wrecking ball is bouncing comical
On the formica of a cracked horizon

Thunder as night falls:
Frightened children grab knives
To slice the stale air
And chase monsters away--
I go back to my rented quarters
Inspired to write the killer saga
Of a beached wail-- you know the tune:
Put some Orca in your Lorca
Slipping slowly off the keys
Spraying sonar grammar
On the rocks

Welcome to the scree of bodies
Voiced, uninvoiced but fully counted
No longer at a discount-- sold on cities--
holding out for a higher resolution

NOBODY HOME
2009

NY/PR, summer

Now watch me as I trip. Tripartite. The blood. The wail. The scar parts.
Rootless, yo, before the age of routers. Yo mismo fui. Rooting for sun in the
gray snow. The potted palms in frozen cities. El salmo sin salida. Sin saliva.
The sin of looking back. And missing the road before me. Eroding expanse.
Can homelands stand, or must they fizzle into mindscape? Now that mothers
live alone and lean against the verandas of endless summers, trying to resist
nostalgia (the passing of time in Time-Life classic 80s soul collections and
confections), where is our birthright, our connection to skin? What do we
have but pop cult flotsam, sampling ringtone beats and boasts? ("Yo no soy,
solo floto-- mi flow ignoto ignites the neurons: identity's remainder. I dent
y tú?") Perhaps the skin is in the synapse. The rest is skeleton and scansion.
They say my drive is low on memory (the coat racks and 8-tracks of childhood
filed away under "missing"). But I'm on the way back to beachfronts that
birthed us (you know the ones with Pizza Huts and zinc roofs side by side?).
Besideness is the only way. No soundtrack b-sides. No fries with that. No
bio. The bio-logical family's deposed. We're no longer "nucular." Now
angles of sunlight stand for belonging. The island's blurred. The city's gassed.
Pero nos queda el goce de estar vivo (contented contigo o con Tego o con
Tivo). Here, in Buzz-Lite City, all meals are to go. All poets are goateed and
blogging to the ether (net cables of oblivion). Staring at ombligos (their own
and others'). Otherwise occupied with staving off the loneliness. Of living
in corporate bones. Awash in 80s reunion specials. The way it never was.
Awash in Swatch. With no past except as fall: as injury. Where is home now?
Home is what you can't flip (no switch, no script, no beachfront condo). You
come up only with platitudes cribbed from postcards: lampposts, boulevards,
governors' mansions with mango trees. The front of manicured yards turned
to shards. Come up only to breathe. Turn to neighbors (made-up) in beds
(unmade) and ask yourself: what now? This is not my island and I am no man
yet. Still a child. Tanta luz. La que no se ve entre tanto gris. Don't call me out
for failing to remember. I'll call you instead. Mi gente'll call tu gente. (No
solo. No Lavoe in Guitar Hero.) We can talk about what to forget next. What
to forgo. Foreground rhythm. Siempre son. If you forget faces, maybe words
will lead you back. To truer senses. Maybe just fences. (Pickets not pictured.)
Un poquito de fractura. Here, in Buzz-Lite City, memoriam's manufactured.
And you know there never was an "in." Where to begin then? Man, you're
fucked if you think there is a method. Forget the scenery. Only unseen now.
Tap into synapse and skin... and ask around: This road leads dónde? Nadie
responde. Write this one down (against Baudelaire): correspondence can only
be picked up far away from home. In a mesh of your own making. Waking
up to trees. After the tremors.

MANCO MUNIDADES

"Nunca hubo sangre en esta historia" - Yara Liceaga

Los abrazos mudos de familias distantes,
Las hogueras y guirnaldas de culturas encontradas
A la hora aplazada del reality programming.

Los antiguos tirapiedras respondieron al llamado
De su actual intervención corporativa
Tomándose unas largas vacaciones
Con el sorbeto insípido del periquero por contrato.

Ahora,
En el anonimato del "off the hook" y el "off the chart",
Las juventudes Wal-mart le dan vueltas al estacionamiento
Confundiendo la costa con el Costco.

Y la abuela "retro" dice:
"Es verdad que nadie les ve las caras a los más hermosos informantes
Pero no importa, porque en época de guerra todos somos performeros:
Todos degustamos la dulce arcilla de civilizaciones."

Las abuelas lo saben todo.
Por eso se te va la voz a la hora de pedir la bendición.

Por eso escribes Manco con mayúscula.

Chris "Chilo" Cajigas

SING ME A SONG

Sing me a song of independence
Threatened by a ship from Spain in 1493
Teach me of Cacique Urayoan
ordering Tainos to drown Diego Salcedo
in a river
all because he
was playing God

sing me a song of African labor in a foreign field
singing songs of Yoruba and mixed blood
mingling with Arawaks in the mountains
sending arrows through the air
sing me a song of the free pirate Robin Hoods like Roberto Cofresi
siempre para la gente

Sing me a song of independence
Cause I can still hear mi gente
gritando en Lares
Primo, sing me a song of Black Puerto Ricans that went to Harvard
Tell me a tale of exiled doctors designing flags
and motivating movements in neighboring islands
My man, is it true how we're happy to fight?
And that the Statue of Liberty has worn the Puerto Rican flag twice?

Sing me a song of hot blood boiling over imperialistic colonialism
that has damaged the psyche of this people
Make me learn of the mass sterilization of my Boricua women
Tell me of sugar cane strikes striving to expose sugar monopolies
and medical experiments sponsored by the Rockefellers
Rant on the radiation from practiced bombings in Vieques
And lament at the absence of a vote in this political system
that decides our economic fate
remind me of revolts in Aguadilla.
As you sing me a poem by a woman named Lola
that was kicked out of her island twice
because of her poetry
show me
Cemented ties
five point stars over aprons in the name of freedom
Explain to me the solemn fee

of being the last colony of an Empire

Let me know why we traded our playground to the U.S. military
And school me on the significance of the shade of blue
in the flags colors

Brother, tell me of a country willing to let me come over legally
As long as they can exploit me cheaply
For my labor
And make me a professional minimum wager
a soldier in their wars, of course
I think it's quite clear,
how we became citizens in 1917, hear here
The U.S.A. drafted 20,000 Puerto Ricans to fight in WW1
that very same year

send me your representatives to rule my land
and make me aware of those executed
for killing European police chiefs in San Juan
after you mention those massacred in oppressive cities
bearing the name of mass murderers like Ponce
Won't they sing about a time when it was illegal in Puerto Rico
to carry a Puerto Rican flag?
Or sing a patriotic tune?
"y lo juro por mi gente, yo juro que mi suerte cambiara"

Ha!
Make me know about the madness
that made martial law manifest in Jayuya
Tell me bout the time they came for President Truman while the White house
was undergoing renovations

Let your statements
Sing me a song of a nation that never was but steady is
One of nationalists opening up fire in the House of Representatives
And getting pardoned by Clinton
Listen
freedom
we've come to tell stories of Clementes and Tito Puentes
of Young Lords in Chicago and New York
Living in churches
taking over hospitals

to demand more money for low-income housing

Clap on a conga and call to my consciousness clearly
To recollect radiation of a real confused culture
reacting with residential bombings
That sing me the symbolism of struggles staged
In the seventies
At Hostos Community College in El Bronx

Mijo, beckon me to Bushwick,
lure me to the lower East Side,
bring me to El Barrio
and we party, yo
and I'll fill you in on why some think Uncle Sam is a sicario
Mira, tell me about the FALN
And the men that carry the machetes
As National Guard planes are burning
To the sounds of Bomba y Plena

Why do Latino gangs wear yellow? in the streets of NYC?
Walking around like we semi free endlessly
pero cántame una canción
how far do we have to go
Wells Fargo
to Castro
from sorrow to hoping for tomorrow
What is this commonwealth doing for the common's wealth?
'Cause I'm seeing nothing but more Puerto Rican obituaries
As tropical shots are fired out the front door at federal agents
For the cause of an island nation
that for five hundred years
has never had
its own
Autonomy

TRIBUTE

Esto es para las leyendas
De mi corazón

The inspiration for my motivation and action
This is for the passion transpired and
The memories of movements

For those that
Gave of self more than they would take
Those that paved the way
I want to say

Thank you
Thank you for preserving this culture
for remaining defiant amongst the vultures
and writing what others wouldn't
For getting in front of audiences and expressing yourselves
For sharing
For representing what you represent
Yes, this is my homage

for the legends of the word
The heroes and sheroes of our sangre
That keeps singing
The known and unknown
From the lovely lands left on Caribbean shores
To the skylines seen by the Royal Chicano air force

For those that used letters to raise armies
And change legislations laws
Battling oppression with heated stanzas
Continually caring consciously for their communities cause
This is for
The lost ones and the last ones
The yo's and the bro's
Loisaida, El Bronx, y El Barrio

This is for the godmothers and godfathers
Of this thing we have here
No words can make it clear enough

What we owe you
For the young lords, old kings
And quintessential queens that
Blessed us with their infinite beauty
In times of cruelty and pain

The voices that carried
Inspiration on their backs
And spears in their teeth
Cracked doors open wider than they'd ever been before

Said this is for
The trailblazers and pioneers
Creating paths to travel on

For you are the reasons why
I pass burning torches of light
To children in the Bronx
And tell them to build cities of redemption
Advise them not to wait
For reservations
Telling them you can manifest your destiny

Yes, you are the reason
My right types in nightly dedication
Long after the left was lost to paralysis
Cause you make me wanna pick up writing utensils
And manufacture masterpieces

Mira, look what these humans have built with their words
Homes and roads for millions to travel
The multitudes and more

this is for the ones that made the sun smile
Those writers that made the ears listen alive
And the artists that made the eyes cry
Summoning enough energy in the atmosphere to make
the four winds circumvent

make no mistake
when I say
that this

is for them and them
For those here in the now and in the past let's
Now take a moment to honor and remember them
And I'm not done
I say it again my friends

Until the stories
Are told and retold
And the names of those that move
many are etched
In stones of the lands
That they speak of

It's unbelievable how the trees sway when you talk
We applaud

We salute
We clap and snap
We tribute

But no ode for you could give its proper due

And may the spirit you embody
Keep on in the hearts of humanity
Siempre

Pa'lante siempre
Mi gente
Gracias
Por todo

ODE TO SANDRA MARÍA ESTÉVEZ

Amidst the tropical downpours
in open fields of Yerbabuena
Where mockingbirds mambo
like spirits in blues towns
Finding their way
along the brushstrokes
of an artist

There is a poet
Who delicately uses portals deliciously
To deliver stories of love and struggle

Where young folks send sentiments in open concert
growing like wildflowers

There is
A mother
a daughter
Christened
In the streets
of a people

A poet

Sharing
words

With young lords and Nuyoricans

Growing up
with stories to tell and islands to remember

a woman
extraordinary confusion
Of what is Borinqueña
Quisqueyana
Africana
This mujer of strength
And passion
Mastery of a written language

That flowed
That flows

From the Bronx streets to the suits of Harvard and Yale
Let them hear her aloud in anthologies
In churches
In museums and schools
Read about her in ethnic studies and Latino literature

Sandra Maria Estévez

an instance acknowledged
For everything you have offered
To my people

Sandra is beauty
Songs of melons
And melancholy history
she crafts poems while you're reciting
easily assimilating essence into a stage set

but this is so much deeper
than a stage set
says she didn't start till college
I think this is lies
With lines seasoned like they were
Doctored by abuela

I've had the honor
of witnessing her radiance
in cultural centers
named after Clemente Soto
and in legendary venues on 3ʳᵈ street

crowned godmother
Of this craft
I walk in
A movement
I breathe in

Authentic in her unforgettable odes
Through seasons

Aguaceros
Pouring down
As the people recite in unison
Focused
Together

possibilities make moments happen
For a peso and a poem
I was placed in a portal
Of powerful pronunciation

Doña,
Your words are worlds
to discover
Where my only wish
Is that others
Will continue to be moved
As I have been
in their presence

AGENT IN THE BLUE SHIRT

we arrived on time
walking through the park
and resting at the benches
under the shade

we talked about community
and the movement
and exchanged emails
and phone numbers
for events that were later to come

he watched us from off to the left of my peripheral
long sleeved light blue collared shirt
I had noticed him there for awhile
watching us
"allí, en la camisa azul "

someone waved at him from time to time
and he would look the other way
he had already moved once
from the first bench he had chosen to sit at
listening and watching
obvious

as we eyed the other direction through the trees
to see the cops watching
right there
in front of the courthouse

it was a sunny day in Brooklyn

slowly people showed up
and they brought the drums
and the songs for the times

the time had come
and he rose
when we left the benches for the street
raising signs
in circles

that spoke of
unfairness

calling out, underneath the sun
beating on the drums
summoning ancestors
to please come
chanting for justice
and freedom

of oppression

LaTasha N. Nevada Diggs

T' URU TAKI (MUD LULLABY)

before there was no inti. no killa.

at the bottom of Titicaca,
the creator slept
one day he awoke and emerged
from the lake
above he found shadow people
not to his liking
and decided to make
some adjustments

he created inti and then killa
he turned all the shadow people
to stone

t'urumanta
        he made us
        in the form of cats
t'urumanta
        then he made us
        in the form of monkeys
t'urumanta
        he made us
        in the form of runa

          the Incas were born.

*Inti, sun; killa, moon; t'urumanta, from
mud; runa, people*

UN MOMENTU

1

It was enough for the blacks, the pardos,
the zambos
to become Catholic in 1614.
It was enough to become   orderly and upright,
to pray hard and repent.
The Archbishop of Lima didn't think so.
In death, black was still black and black
could not rest beside a Spaniard
in the cathedral's graveyard.
The city council agreed and remembered
one other item.

Your African ancestry disqualified you for a coffin.
Only a Spaniard could have a coffin.
You, had your sheet, your tattered wool pants;
your hole in the earth
Your swollen body floating back to Africa.

There is no word in Quechua for a black person.

2

The sumaq zamba abandoned home
and became black.
It was easier this way. Easier to be free;
to locate herself.
But easy is too easy to explain her situation.

All this talk over crimes of passion…
How lovely it was to have her sisters,
                    zambo and mulata, as bed flesh.

There is no word in Quechua for a black person.

(It's said they fuck like jackrabbits.)
1574. No black woman shall wear
silk pearls gold or mantillas.
1622. No black woman shall bring

a rug or cushion to sit on in church.
1623. No black woman shall wear
silver bells on their slippers.

No black woman shall wear slippers.

There is no word in Quechua for a black person.

No black woman shall have a canopied bed.
The fruits of prostitution. Tanqay away memory.

So says the Crown.
Says the municipal authorities
when they seized her pretty jewels.

Having been married to a Spaniard
these past two years meant nothing.

*sumaq, pretty; zamba, a person of Indian and African blood;
tanqay, to push*

OMENS, 1781 (VOC DE MICEALA)

that morning ... I found a snake ... in our home ... I killed it

quickly

I lifted my skirt ... and pissed ... upon it ... with bare feet ...

I crushed it

but which foot works better? ... the right ... or the left?

tonight ... I called you the moon ... your hair surrounds
your face ... blue black ... how the stars are flickers ... from the river

beside our incinerated home ... we are ashes ... sacrilege
they split us ... then hang us ... no one is left to covet our remains

they won't allow ... our flesh ... to return to our father ... my love
... did we speak too proudly?

SEÑOR TUPA,

thank you for granting me permission
to respond to your illustrations;
fascinating items have emerged.

on one particular occasion, a woman   rather
the remains of a woman,
visited me in a dream

at first   she was scattered ash floating atop a river.
into the air she lifted like a flock of winged ants

she motioned towards a plaza.   the ants then divided
into groups and transformed into limbs.

the largest group became a torso with its head.
raised from burning wood, the limbs rested upon pikes
and by some force greater than any god we've known,
the pikes displaced themselves in public and frequented places.

Tinta   Quisicanchis   Carababya   Arequipa

her skin   badly bruised   did not hide her blood orange hue.
she   if were it not for divisions of flesh and tendon,   was beautiful

the eyes of honey and coca leaves combined were fearless
her lips full and swollen by circumstance were polished in scarlet
the hair on her head tattered coarse obsidian locks
reflected in Inti's glow traces of her age

as I stood there in the center of the plaza   I saw all her parts
they wrangled on their pedestals or iron demanding audience
they wanted me to know her

they told me her name was Micaela.

sincerely,

tochtli tekpatl, 2008

Roberto F. Santiago

SAVE THE DATE

As I march down that aisle,
I want no music to be played.
I want to savor each step
swaying hips
into figure eights
that no longer need
rhythmic accompaniment because they,
themselves are rhythm
and blues. I want the sound of chiffon and white to carry me
to him. I want to feel every stitch
hum hymns that glide across daddy's stern face
into the clasped hands that give us 'six months at most.'

Mother and the woodless winds
will break into spontaneous sobs. As I pass
their asthmatic arias paint the parish
black and gold. My veil will dance.
Shooting sparks along imperfections,
of the church grey and white marble,
my train will thunderclap as it enters the 14th station.

The choir will be beadwork
so intricate that their harmonies will echo years of experience
and the underpaid self-assuredness that has died
and been dyed again to my specifications.
I will conduct every breath
so that the choir's incantations can be launched
to the balcony on high
where the organist will be sitting
arms crossed- a paid spectator.
And the percussion will be
the soft slick sliding of glass slippers
on a mile-long carpet,
redder than the blood
of any Christ
you've ever lain
your grievances upon.

I'M SURPRISED THERE'S NOT MORE RELIGIOUSLY INFLUENCED EATING DISORDERS

Breakfast,
Altoids and Aquafina.

I'm a tightrope walker
with limited depth perception.
Wearing velvet gender
and bending crystals
I soar above the crowds.
Their hungry mouths agape
I feed them awe.
I'm not a wrestler.
I can't weigh the ropes down.

Lunch,
Aspirin and an Apple.

Gluttony is for the sinner.
The sinner is for the weak.
This isn't a suicide note.
I would never pour myself
onto page
into ink.
Suicide is too naked,
open to interpretation
and wasteful.
I love my self
enough to live.
I'm fasting. I'm disciplined.
To induce
release,
A teenaged Saint Catherine
purified herself
with a twig.
Holy is the restraint.

Another aspirin,
this time with codeine.

I remember wondering how they could do it.

Not eat. I would test my limit everyday.
It was not easy. It is not easy.
To pass the ads, the value meals
to pretend to be a vegan
reading the Anatomy of Melancholy during
Holiday dinners.
It's just chicken.
C'mon it's Christmas!
You're a guy!
You don't have to diet!
I'm not a wrestler!
I cannot weigh the ropes down!

Dinner,
Champagne, Percocet, and an Empty Stomach.

Depression was once known as Sloth.
Sloth is for the sinner.
The sinner is for the meek
and the meek shall inherit the earth
or so they say. When I was younger
I wanted to be a bird.
Feathery, light, and arrogant.
That is why I walk the line
in sequined fuchsia plumage.
That is why my family stopped
coming to the circus.

I HAVE NEVER BEEN LOYAL

Did you expect me to be the dog?
Sitting on the shore rocks, nose upturned,
drinking in the salty air...
all as I waited for you?
All of San Juan at my paws,
but you expect me to wait by the sea
feet firmly planted as the sea foam chokes back
whimpers and tears. Panting, as my fur
  thickens and sheds
into seashells and small fish
until the seasons change and I become stone.

BREATHALYZER

Today, I will find mom in her rose garden.
Pretending to be two smashed strawberries
hiding behind a not-so-white picket fence,
I will lay next to her.

Underneath our orange blossomed sky,
her face is soft and red.
Her hair is hay
or dead grass.
Golden straw- newly spun. Keys
glitter into glowing ornaments extending her long slender branches.

Sometimes
I dream that I am
working in a sardine cannery.
I cut the heads off the fish
until they want me to do it fast,
faster
and so fast
that I worry the world
cannot eat them
fast enough.

Tomorrow, she will find me.

SELF-PORTRAIT OF A BOY KICKED OUT OF
HIS HOUSE

Look at me.

I am Tennessee Williams in a poodle skirt,
crying shame into Grandma's [in] famous coquito.
Filled to the tiptop
of a tea cup
with the gold rim   chipped off.

Is it strange at seventeen to feel that time is running out?

The Hickey-necked boy wonders aloud
on the platform
of the 6 train
going downtown,
head over rails,

There is no good you can do
at 3 in the morning that you couldn't do
at 3 in the afternoon.

But it wasn't the time.
It was the time difference between Castle Hill and Christopher Street.
So, Momma smacked the curfew out of him.
Not listening
Cheek stinging
and don't you ever come back still ringing in my ears.

In the village, I can almost see paradise but I feel
the blue piano kiss my tongue
and it smells too sweet
to have no taste.

Who am I kidding?

I'm more like a
not-so-Blanche Dubois
giving away my Belle Rêve to any
body willing
to pretend that sunrise isn't an emergency
                              exit.

Frank Pérez

RHYTHM OF LIFE

In the name of the clave, maraca and holy bongo-
Ache'.
In the beginning, there was rhythm.
From the fiery flames of Africa to the cool Caribbean breeze
There was rhythm.
From the bloody swords of the conquistadores,
To the lush guitar strings of Pedro Flores,
There was rhythm.
From the Taino test of Uroyoan
To the tropical projects of St. Ann's
There was rhythm.
From the blood-stained earth of the men, women and children
of the Ponce massacre,
To the tear stained flag and cry of "Libre" del
Grito de Lares,
There was rhythm.
From the primal screams of Albizu for "freedom"
from the chains that bind us,
To the mambo mentality, Café con Leche, Ron con Coke,
Pasteles-reality that defines us,
There was rhythm.
From the Bomba y Plena waves of Luquillo beach.
To the gua-guan-co of guitar-shaped Latinas of Orchard beach,
There was rhythm.
From Hector's battle cry of "Mi Gente! . . . Ustedes!"
To Eddie's sweet smell of "Cafe...tostao y colao."
There was rhythm.
From Re-pression, De-pression and Op-pression
Came the jam session!
And they came...
Afri-can, Puertori-can, Nuyori-can, Domini-can, Mexi-can,
Jamai-can, Nosotros-can, We-can, Latinos-can!
When we came, we told our story thru the drum,
Then via "Radio Bemba"- "Bochinche!" Word of mouth!

The words you have heard are all true.
No names have been changed to protect the innocent.
Because there are none, we're all guilty.
Today, we shall find out if it takes S.P.I.C.s,
AKA- Special People of International Character

To see the beauty of the spoken word and realize the
fact that, you, me and we, are the Rainbow Trinity.
In the name of the clave, maraca and holy bongo- Ache'.

SPOKEN WORD OR POETRY

Many people ask is Spoken Word Poetry?
Or is Poetry Spoken Word?

Here are some types of Poetry and Spoken word that I've heard.

I am the traditional Orator!
I speak my words ar-ti-cu-late-ly.
The Old School way of Poetry
My words are like speeches.
Sometimes I speak too long and make you say "Jesus."

I am the Mellow Poet.
I speak in mellifluous prose.
Like a rose, my words are soft and smooth
and when you hear them, they make you... go... ooooh.

I am the ranter and the raver!
I rant and I rave to save the earth.
I rant and I rave because I feel the urge!
I rant about this...
I rave about that...
I rant to rave
I rave to rant
I rant and rave until I can't.

I am the Memorizer!
The memorizer bunny
I will dazzle you with how many words are in my memory.
I will hit you with words and images,
images and words, words and words.
Lengthy explanations all to show how many words I can keep in me
Do I have message? Hmmm . . . Let me see.
Nope
I'm just the memorizer bunny always talking about Me, Me, Me.

Spoken Word _is_ poetry.
We're all part of the same literary tree.
Poetry is Spoken Word,
And Spoken Word is me.

THE CREED

I believe in me, myself, and I.
I believe I will run at the first sign of you and me.
I believe that no one in this world is worthy of me.
And that I, definitely don't deserve anybody.
I believe in living for the moment and love of life.
I believe in make-up sex, Hennessey, blunts and long hazy nights.
I believe in me being me and living life to the fullest day to day.
I answer to no one, get up when I want, and say what I want to say.
Whether it stresses people or causes strife,
I don't give a fuck, cause it's my Life!

THE MAN IN BLACK

His words flow;
His mind goes
His eyes roll.
As the original (shadowy figure) man in black,
sets up to attack

"Woke up this morning, feeling excellent"

The Literal liberator of New York's Puerto Rico;
The Emancipator of Puerto Rican angst;
The "cuentero" or storyteller of the journey de
Mami y Papi on the Marine Tiger.
Through our Boricua Bible…The Puerto Rican Obituary
And the words of wisdom flow again…

"To be a poet, you have to remain single forever,
with someone who will never let you go"

A mentor to some, partner in crime to others and his
street wisdom continues…

"The best way to teach children about poetry is by
keeping your mouth shut and listening to what they
have to say."

So if you think you're a Poet, check out the man in black
What he did and what he wrote to put it articulately "ain't whack."
So cooperate, collaborate, fornicate, commiserate, celebrate, communicate,
Do it now before it's too late.
Don't let Pedro's words go to waste.

His shoes are too big to fill
so don't try you'll just get ill.
With the last line unwritten,
And no time to finish the last rhyme
The poem remains un-done
The book remains open
Our work here has begun…
"Woke up this morning, feeling, feeling, feeling…"

Sheila Maldonado

POOL

Words have not held me up like that water does. I would like them to try,
acquire a density that changes gravity, changes how I think of me, if I think of
me. There, I see blue, make breath into bubbles, let my arms become my legs.
My body remembers how to be every time I step into that dimension of flow and
glide. The water gets up in every crack of me, possessive, quietly, the way I like
it. I thought it would let me go when I jumped in the deep end the first time,
but it wrapped itself around me, inside me. I closed my lips, opened my eyes,
my arms, and met its surface. Here, I wind toward a bottom I
can't see. I flail about trying to catch a current, an
                    embrace.I don't know how I'll rise
                  again, how this will deliver
                     the breath I need.

HOMEBODY

I got this place so I could be naked,
lotion up after a shower, no rush
to throw on a robe or sleep clothes, to cover
myself so my brother, father, mother
don't catch me, think I'm a freak getting off
on their living room couch while they're asleep.

They swear I got this place so I can sleep
with any dude off the street, strip him naked,
have my man-eating way and send him off.
I wish I were the kind that got a rush
from conquest, but I'm more like my mother,
too beat to get out from under the covers.

This place is my refuge, where I recover
from the world, elude angry sleepwalking
drones who act like they have no mother.
I'm my own child here, dancing bare-ass nekkid,
don't care if the neighbors see a rush of
skin from their window, my body taking off.

I know my mother wishes she could slack off
like me, have her own place to take cover.
The house of men she keeps threatens to crush
her daily. She finds space only in her sleep,
where she dreams of an all-white house, clean, naked.
She's done with dirty men who need a mother.

I squeezed out of there before I got smothered.
Let them say what they like, their words roll off
my shell. It's safe to be tender, naked
in here. I might invite someone to uncover
me every once in a while. I can't sleep
alone always. I'm compelled to brush

against other flesh, feel its weight crush
me open. I can't fight urges my mother
does, disconnect from my body in sleep.
But I don't accept too many offers,
there's still too much of me undiscovered,

truths for my eyes only, hidden in nakedness.

I won't uncover anything if I rush.
In this sleepy cave, I can mother
myself, peel off burdens 'til I'm naked.

FUTURE TENSE (MINOR TRIBE: 2012)

like the family
I need documents to stay here
lose them and I lose my place

this is the right place, right?
this is where I'm supposed to be?

Rumi thinks your country
is where you're headed
not where you are

Tomás says we never arrive

we're smuggled in the back of a truck
riding anonymous in the dark
thru the middle of a place
that doesn't want us

wants only pieces of us

we come in pieces

pottery shards
temple fragments
stone bits

imagining blood
in different cities

cities of us
abandoned

we didn't die
we hid

what was remembered
wasn't put down
on rock
on paper

so that it could be smashed
so that it could be burned

I became unrecognizable
dulled easily in the meanwhile
between peaks and valleys

already I'm from a people so small
we might be overlooked
when the end comes

it's hard prying us open
but there are ways to make us talk

I thought my generation
escaped silence

it came back for me

severed me from a tongue
that once spoke like a mirror
revealed exits

when I got quiet
I opened a door onto
a maze of space

I drifted
hurting myself
banging into unseen borders

I'm from folks who
used to know their way around
the universe

at the very least
they knew people
who knew people
who knew the way

the only thing I could do
was make a chain

a line of letters
to anchor me
back to my vessel

I'm still adrift
but it's a new floating
a purpose whispering behind it

cycle breaking
avoiding ends
disguised as paths

I got 9 years
and about 6 months
left to explore

THE NEGATIVE REPRESENTATION OF SHEILAS
IN THE MEDIA

Thanks to Ready for the World,
people have mocked me since
sixth grade, "Oh, Oh, Oh, Oh
Sheila" sung humping, like

a dog on a leg. From then on,
I became acutely aware of the
popular portrayal of my name and
all its hookerish connotations.

Some more examples:
On *Midnight Marauders*, one of
Tribe Called Quest's albums, Phife,
horny, calls up one of his "hooker
hos, oh yo, Sheila's home;"

On *Frasier*, Roz, the show slut, poses
as a Sheila, the sleazy other woman,
to help Frasier's father make the
lady he's been seeing jealous;

In *Virtuosity*, a Denzel/Russell Crowe
movie where they're virtually real,
a program called Sheila 2.1
is basically a computer skank.

The last straw:
On *Will and Grace*,
thinking up baby names
in the sperm insemination office
Sheila comes up but Will says,
"Sheila's a whore's name."
The nurse in the room protests,
"That's *my* name, but I am a whore."

An exception:
Sheila E., an actual Sheila singing
honestly of hos on "The Glamorous Life"
turned it around, actually does work,

is a real musician, can really play
the drums, the timbales, the conga
all at once, can channel misunderstood
sexual energy in order to rock a crowd.

Finally, a role model.

AT THE MEER IN HARLEM

There is a dark reflection that is pulling me into another world. A wavy
impressionistic Monet world. An upside-down tower Alhambra world. It's
a brown sky plus orange street light equals purple night. To my right, there's
a couple kissing on a bench. Kissing a bench. Someone should be kissing
tonight. It's an early fake spring. It's me with me in the dark park hoping
no one will be stabbing me. No one should be. It feels too cozy mellow for
stabbing. If it were to happen, it would just be aesthetically inappropriate.
That criminal would have done a disservice to his/her art. That's what I would
tell him/her. It's not a night for that. Make out the ducks in the middle of
the ripple, stabber. Avoid the raccoon silhouette on the garbage can. Count
the orbs of traffic signal lamppost light, yellow, red, white in the bizarro water.
Take in the green smoke.

John "Chance" Acevedo

ART OF MAKING LOVE

Cuatro inebriated rings
Maybe drunk body
will write you a sober poem
Careful how you use your mouth
Your speech feels good
Wonder how often you work on your diction
Your tongue needs to be strong
See your words weigh heavy on my heart
Your breath feels like fingertips
I'm touched
by the way you speak to me so please,
Sentence me a comforter for these cold nights
Imitate intimacy on scrabble boards so our words connect
Let metaphors commit suicide so their souls connect
Hold conversations on holograms so you can see
what switching topics looks like
I like to think we fornicate with each others brain
So we orgasm after sharing thoughts
Blank stares are fixed on you like naked canvas
Canvas your naked body with stares
Step on stairs to make it to the level you are on
I day dreamed about our first kiss
Let the residue of our embrace
Be used for the next oil painting
Let's sweat our next master piece in some way
Or piece together what masters
Tried to make us sweat away
Crack that whip to motivate our commitment
Let's commit to sestina a child together
and hold it above our heads like the chapel
After we take our time
and Mona Lisa our love for each other
Let it take us time to produce perfection
Van Gogh a son
Call out to the stars and let Galileo hear you
With patient hands let's Marquez our vows
Trujillo any situation we may run into
Neruda and Hughes our life
Start something new with each breath we write into existence
Frida a daughter

Minus the unibrow
What I'm saying is
Let's make art since fucking is so easy to do

MOMENT OF SILENCE

I didn't choose you, my heart did
And he's looking at you to be the person that can help him remove the last
name he tattooed on it
I just wish I was able to get you out of my head
But like my mothers name that is just hard to do
I don't want you to be a twin but wish that I saw double
when looking at you
Eres preciosa como el arco iris después de la lluvia
Estoy en pas contigo
eres las brezas de la noche que pasan en el verano
el remedio que necesita el corazón partido
Solo quisiera vivir un siglo si se que la pasare junto a ti
Ton sourire illumine les cœurs et donne naissance a l'espoir.
ca devrait un crime d'aimer autant comme je t'aime
Let this thing in my chest
Relay messages to this thing in my head in whatever language
Produce this poem in Braille so the blind can slide their fingers and understand
what being with you feels like.
We approached this like NYC transit slow,
with hearts in need of repair,
so I apologize that it takes me so long to come on the weekends.
But when I get there, it's all worth the wait.
We can move to Seattle
I can show them how cloudy days mean nothing
when someone brightens up your life
An eclipse can't cast shadows on this feeling
I don't ever want to be in the dark about you
so I try not to sleep- ok that's a lie
but I'll sleep after you and wake up before you
so that I don't miss you as much
I only leave you to go to work
My heart needs no GPS to find its way back to you
It recognizes you
Like Nike signs, blackberry icons, superman's logo, horrible fashion statements,
major league baseball and blue and white pinstripes
Like purple and gold to NBA, bells to Pavlov's dog,
Like hookers to the point
The point is
getting you out of my system
Is really hard to do

So I guess I can sum up
all that I want to say
by being cliché
And those 3 little words-
I love you.

OVERCOMING DV

Run
Run as if you were waiting for salvation on the other side of that wall.
Don't look back
Questioning is what got you the night at the hospital, so I say run
Run like
Africans in marathons that need this win to save starving villages in Nigeria,
Senegal, Angola,
Let wind caress body as you cut through
Don't hesitate
Hesitating is what got you the broken jaw
So run with confidence pretty lady
Don't allow your face to be introduced to his four finger ring
You don't have to read his name in the mirror anymore
Spread your wings beautiful.
Let the sounds of flutes move you
Remember them as freedom
Kick down depression
Walk over bad memories
As you run past the
still trees that home red and gold leaves
from 86 to 96 street
Past pictures on billboards that remind you of self pity
Run past the stores filled with disguised compliments and reassurance
Don't allow yourself to be the wolf that licks razors
and tastes his own blood
His sugar coated words shouldn't cause you to run back to him
Instead I say run with your back to him,
run and listen differently
hear in broken silence
allow the music to transport you to the yesterdays of happiness
Como el polvo que se barre debajo la alfombra
recuérdate que siempre hay polvo
siempre hay alfombra.
Different escobas and that you will be great
Because you meant it like writing with pen that sheds blood
so you can't put some of you in everything you write and then maybe one day
you can finally breathe and walk.

SIP NIP SNIP

She never liked drinking
It was really for social occasions
Until drinking became the sole motivation that
Helped him from convincing and start persuading
She never knew how fermented grapes or aged fruits could be intoxicating.
He must have had a minor in hospitality
It explains how well mannered he would become when boys in blue asked questions about
Domestic disturbance
"No sir, no issues here"
Her screams are silenced
By the language barrier
Because policemen in this neighborhood
No hablan español after 6 and
He knew they would look for black and blues
So he placed force that'll go undetected
By a physicians first site
this is why doctors touch
But not like he touched
He touched with blind folded heart
Like he never seen her before
like she stole from him
Like she was an enemy
Like he prepared for months for this fight
like he's not responsible for my 2 siblings
like he had a personal punching bag
But She never nipped it
She allowed his
threats of self-destruction
manipulate her happiness
His "I can't do this without you"
Is the reason why he can still
Make a guest appearance in her heart
Even though a broken jaw line
and bloody bandages
Remind her not to
Maybe if she nipped it,
Her daughter's therapist and son's flashbacks would be nonexistent
Maybe if she nipped it the first time he tried to use his fist
we wouldn't be going through this

3 oral/dental surgeries
1 replaced jaw line
2 ensuring that gums will hold teeth
And a cleansing so she can smile pretty again
2 foot surgeries- 1 for each foot- to help her walk away from these men that
don't treat her as they should
1 heart transplant to help her love her three children the way she loved looking
at the bottom of empty bottles
Maybe men
like dawgs
with too much pent up aggression need to have their balls snipped.
Maybe then, they'll think twice about how they treat women.

Machete Movement

THE POETS

El David & Machete Movement

Without us, the world is flat and the sun is God
Without us, there are no revolutions and there is no hope
Without us, there are no scriptures,
No torah, no Koran, no revelations
Without us, CNN is King and the fascists are good
The left wing is the right wing and the right wing is the left

Without us, the world is dark and the people are blind
Without us, the universe does not exist
and the world is two-dimensional
Without us, Killer cops are heroes and Killer presidents are loved

Without us, radical words are imprisoned in the mind
And the mind is only free because we free our words
And it is because we free our words that revolutionaries have a voice
And it is because revolutionaries have a voice
that there are winds of change
And the winds of change blow away the curtains
and the masks that conceal the evil of man
And it is because the evil of man is revealed that the unjust is fought
And it is fought because the power of the people
Rises like the phoenix from the ashes
Warriors march forward and victory is in sight
Peace is in sight
Justice is in sight
Because of us

We are the tellers of truth
We are the revolutionaries of words…words…words…

We give you our minds
We give you our hearts
And we give you our souls

Thought is creative and we are the thinkers
Exhausting ammunition from our mind; exploding on paper
And published to the world
What the universe whispers in our ears we shout from the rooftops
We are the exercisers of the last freedom….thought

We are…the poets

ABUELITA
El David & Machete Movement

Abuelita - Mama Kinta
What would she do?
What would she say?
If Abuelita could see... what I see
Abuelita would freak
she would break down and cry out in pain
Ashamed – cuz' there was no fight sustained
There was no fight to be free –
If Abuelita could see

Abuelita, African, and Boricua
Raised on Arawak land, occupied and captive by the Spanish Crown
A Black woman with Taino blood
Speaking a foreign tongue but
Never losing her own
Never forgetting her home
From the sacred hills of Yucahu to the African Quimbambas
Both tattooed in her heart and soul
Born from the womb of a slave...surviving through hell
Mama Kinta never forgot the struggle the pain,
the whips and the chains
Never forgot that freedom is not free
And that she would always be one step away from slavery
So she stood strong in all that she did

Abuelita sat outside el bohío on the old wooden rocker
Piercing eyes forever watching
Lips tight and chin up high like a warrior chief
In her right hand the machete, always ready
Her left hand habitually rubbing the rough lines
on the back of her neck
Dead tissue- remnants of the oppressors whip
Scars of war and each scar a folk lore
So, Abuelita Mama Kinta, conditioned to be hard
Even in her laughter...ha! Ha! ha!
She loved her black brothers and sisters
Loved her brown brothers and sisters
Persecuted chained and whipped
Never would you hear the word nigger pass her lips

Abuelita Mama Kinta so strong and bold
Even when so many in her time sold out their own
Aiming at their own, holding the oppressors gun
Abuelita Mama Kinta did not run
She took her whips for the race
She bled, she cried and she nearly died before she was free
And Abuelita Mama Kinta did that for me
And for you- so that we could stay free

But if Abuelita Mama Kinta could see the world today
Her people gone astray
living for the lust instead of living for the day
What would she say? What would she do?
If Abuelita could see her young brothers pumping poison into the veins of
their own community
Seeing their sister as a sale and a quick buck
And providing her with white stones that kill her
slooooooowly but surely
Her life bought his gear,
her blood bought his whip and the rims on it

If Abuelita could see her young people taking their music,
A child of the spiritual Bomba and Bata drums,
And lacing it with perversion and evil
Advocating black on black crime
Man, if Abuelita could see,
Our people using a word that she heard many times before someone would get
beat, whipped, lynched and killed
as a term of endearment
If she could see young brothers and sisters
wearing chains and earrings of platinum, gold and ice
Pimping themselves to the children
of the same demons that had enslaved her

So what would she say?
I believe it would be…
No! I am not your nigger!
I am your mother and I survived long enough for you
and your parents to be born
I gave you the gift of freedom
I paid for that gift with my blood, sweat, tears and with my life
And you used that gift to take us back…

Back to the hell we struggled to be free of
You take us back to hell, back to oppression and back to slavery
Back to hell
No! I am not your nigger...
I am your mother...Abuelita Mama Kinta

And that's what I believe she would say if she was able to see today

AMERICA'S BRAINCHILD

El David & Machete Movement

America-
I am the effect of your cause
The side effect, the 1% chance of failure
I am the evidence of oppression
The evidence of hate
The result of a prolonged oppressive state

I am the amazing story
The fall from grace, to the rising of the sun
I was born from your flames
But I did not disintegrate- I was refined, purified

America-
I was made stronger by the flames you ignited
The world was on fire, but from the ashes I rose
I am of the good, not a pacifist, but good
The good that was tested by flames
The rough rock holds no reflection

You burned me in your fire
Then I was refined and polished
So that Chango could see his image in me
So that the image of Chango could be reflected
So that I would be the reflection of Chango
The King who would reclaim his throne

America-
You made me
You gave me poison to drink and diseases to hold
You gave me heroin, dust, cocaine, and crack rocks
You cuffed my hands and feet in chains
You gave me lashes from whips, and white blood to shrink my lips
So that I would fade from black to brown and from brown to tan and from tan
to white
You kept telling me to,
"Stay down, nigger stay down Spic…Stay Down"
But how could I
When I was gold, and your flames just made me stronger
Your fires just made me more beautiful

More immune to pain,

You gave me the back of the bus
You gave me small reservations in my own home
You gave me the feel of your sword, your guns, and your bombs
You gave me your drugs, your diseases, your spit, your guilt
You gave me your left over's, your material lust, your waste and filth
Then you told me to wash it away by drinking from your holy book

But the Gods from your holy book were asleep
They did not come down to dance with you
They did not come down to advise you
And they did not warn you that we were not defeated...that we were not down
and out
That we were soldiers inside the wooden horse
Slowly picking apart your world
You did not know
That it was Olofi behind the image of your savior
That it was Chango behind the image of your lady in red
That it was Obatala behind the image of your lady in white
That it was Elegua behind the image of your holy child

America-
I grew stronger from your hatred, your racism, and your genocide
I grew stronger from your diseases and your globalization
For it was your occupation, your action, your hate and oppression that woke
me up
That woke *US* up

It was your fire lit under us that made us unite and take a stand
You gave us a reason to seek the thunder and fire of Chango and the sword of
Ogun

America-
It was you...it was you
Mother Fucker it was you!
You made me
I am the effect of your cause

Welcome to your Brainchild

Lisa Alvarado

BASHERT

I am the catch
in your throat;
the wordless cry,
unexplainable.

I am the cloud
that follows you;
raining
at the slightest provocation.

I am the scar
that has
become a flower.

I am the pilgrim
you brought home;
the Jew you hid
from the fire.

I am your dark sleep.

I am your dream
of finding someone
whose arms
will hold you
when daylight comes.

HOMECOMING

Pour eternity
into the Kiddush cup tonight
Drink, drink, drink,
Each drop's
a memory revealed.

I slake my thirst
with the breath of angels
and ancestors,
and taste Sephardi
on the tip of my tongue.

I will dance this Shabbat
with a rose
blooming from my lips,
a star in each eye.
Moonlight,
a ribbon in my hair.

COURTING DISASTER

I'm washing the dishes and I hear the key turning in the lock, his footsteps coming toward me. I'm at the sink and I'm in no hurry to finish; it's not like I don't know why he's here. Besides, he's early, and he can just be a good boy and wait. But he's not a good boy and I know it.

We're up to twice a week now and have been for the last month. I'm not quite sure how it happened, but somehow, we've got the keys to each other's apartment. It's not to be confused with access to each other's lives. The rules are: a brief phone call in the morning, yes or no, where and when, and then it's just a matter of time.

The water is finally coiling its way down the drain and I wring out the dishrag and sponge. He doesn't ask me how I am or say hello. But I feel him close behind me, and then his hands rest on my shoulders, and his mouth latches onto the nape of my neck, mouth hot on my skin. I lean back a little and his hands slide down my arms and trail their way to my waist. He licks at me, working his way to my earlobe. He takes the flesh between his teeth and bites down. I manage to stay still until then, but that bright, little pain pushes me over the edge. "Yes," I breathe, "Yes...now."

He turns me around and unbuttons my shirt, shoves up my bra and begins to thumb my nipples around and around like time passing, like time chasing its tail. I feel them harden and now I want to touch him somewhere else, make him hard somewhere else, make time turn in on itself, start and stop and dissolve.

The kitchen stays silent. I'm always quiet, no matter what. I only talk to him this way, with flesh, with skin answering skin. His hands find the zipper of my pants, make it move, find their way between my legs where he's allowed to know my small, hard secret--the only secret I will ever tell him.

His fingertips wetly trace time's unraveling against the edges of the slick wet skin. Slowly, around and around, and then just for a minute I stop to look at his face, softer and younger than mine. My eyes travel their way to his -- dark, sullen, deep. I think I can see myself in them, but then he blinks and says, "I know you're close now."

His fingers move again, simple, simple circle--the circle erasing everything, blotting out the minutes, collapsing the hours. I start to shake against him, close my legs against his hand. I shatter and I want him to feel the waves of it, draw it into himself through the tips of his fingers.

When he's finished, I slowly take his hand and lick away the taste, honey-sweet, salty as tears, bitter as ash. We say nothing as he leans close, swiping his lips across mine.

"Now me," he says, and reaches to pull off his belt. I put my hand over his, "No," I whisper.

"Not here. Come lie down with me," and I lead the way toward the bedroom. We're silent again, no sound except our footsteps, the sound of our breath. Then I hear him.

"What I wouldn't do for you," he sighs. "Don't," I say, "don't ruin it for me."

A. B. Lugo

VOICES AT EL MORRO

Shhh—
If I'm real quiet,
I can hear their voices.

They come in threes
Three voices,
three languages,
three prayers

Xan xan katú
Ashé
Amén

My maiden voyage
to my motherland,
standing in El Morro,
the castle-fort at the
northwestern tip of Old San Juan,
I hear their voices

I hear the singing of the Taíno
the melody of their final *areito*
I feel the drumming of the Yoruba
in the beating of my heart
I see the dancing of the Spaniard
in the flapping of the hoisted flags
swirling around,
fierce winds
whipping through me
atop this
architecturally-beautiful
killing machine

Through indentured servitude,
slavery and serfdom,
El Morro and its surroundings
have come to epitomize
the extremes of my life,
my people
White - black

The bricks now sullied with soot
and years of regret
Rich - poor
Vibrant colors of Old San Juan
side by side
with muted colors
and decrepitude of
neighboring La Perla
Life - death
The metal used to make the cauldron
of sustenance for the soldiers
the same
as the cannonballs used
to destroy the enemy

My reverie disrupted,
my pilgrimage interrupted
by the flashing and clicking
of a disposable camera
A father and son
posing for and
taking photographs

Couldn't these tourists
feel the pain
in these walls?
Hear the wailing
in the seas?
Smell the death in the air?
Do they even care?

El Castillo San
Felipe del Morro
fought off
invaders for centuries
I'm fighting the
voices of ghosts
in my head
The voices are continuing,
all speaking at the same time

Xan xan katú

Ashé
Amén
Xan xan katú
Ashé
Amén

If I'm real, real quiet,
I can hear the voices
of my ancestors
welcoming me home

GHETTO NOSTALGIA (PALADINO AVENUE)

Paladino Avenue
is between the FDR Drive
and what we called "Crack Park"
Paladino Avenue—
the avenue that goes backward
The numbers of its buildings
increase from north to south,
not the other way around
like its neighbor First Avenue
Naked,
no lane markings
Narrow yet defiantly remaining a two-way street
It rebels against the grid system
of Manhattan streets,
curving its three-block length
as it refuses to play it straight

I stand on Paladino Avenue
and I am transported back to simpler days
Back when we played on
jungle gyms so unsafe
they could kill us
and we lived for the danger
Days of Manhunt and dodgeball
giving way to asphalt basketball in the summer
and street football in the winter
where instead of the instant replay,
we had the do-over
Back when rappers didn't die—
they only faded into obscurity,
making room for the next class of street poets
Back to days of spelling bees and assemblies,
honor guard and carrying the flag,
pledges of allegiance and not knowing
what it all stood for or meant
Back when Saturday nights were filled
with SNL and Apollo and
whatever else was on TV
Back when you couldn't hang out too late
or else face Miss Antoinette on the ninth floor

who was on Tenant Patrol
and you know she would tell your mama

Back in those days when
Watchie was still Jorge,
Nancy, Nadine, and Edna
were the *bochincheras* of P.S. 112 and 206—
three Gorgons of gossip
Lucy the epitome of new Latina cool
her pixie cut dyed blonde,
short, poom-poom shorts
and attitude for days
Back when Armando, Saulo, and Shondu were my boys
The only wars we knew were between
Section 1 on First Avenue
and Section 2 on Second
The only guns we had were Super Soakers
that could seemingly spray water for miles
The only drugs we did
were Spanish coffee and the ink
on rexograph, mimeograph sheets
in the days before Xerox
and sex was something we talked about
but didn't do
and if we did
the worst that could happen
was you got a girl pregnant

Watchie sells drugs now, or so they say
Nancy and Edna became mothers at a young age
Nadine's fate even worse—
she became a cop
Lucy died of AIDS,
and I don't even speak to Saulo,
Shondu or Armando anymore
Super Soakers gave way to nine-millimeters,
Saturday Night Live gave way to Saturday Night Specials,
which gave way to killing our own
which gave way to choke holds and wallets
and candlelight vigils
which gives way to me
waxing nostalgic for days long gone

Days when ignorance was bliss
and happiness could be had
when we had a substitute teacher
on inclement weather days
or when we ran to the *piragüero*'s cart
or the icee truck in the summertime

Ghetto nostalgia takes over me
I become dumbfounded
as I stand on Paladino Avenue—
the street of my youth
Paladino Avenue—
the avenue that goes backward
There I stand,
silently hoping that
I go backward with it

PIETRI POETRY
Dedicated to El Reverendo Pedro Pietri and nobody else

Pedro always had his head in the clouds
The view was better from up there
Dropping bits of wisdom
in an insane reality
He went to war
and when he came back
went to war again
on his adopted soil
words his weapon of choice

Clad always in black
with long, flowing curly locks
and a smile that knew more
than it was letting on
Pedro walked the line
walked the rooftops
looking for salvation
He did what came naturally
went to church

With a basket of *tomates*
El Reverendo preached in his *iglesia*
teaching us it was all right
to take the language
of two oppressors and create our own:
Spanglish

Words flowed
finding their way
to pages
and books
and libraries
to places where
the masses are asses
and it doesn't matter
if Jesus is leaving
we would always find him
in *el livingroom*

con artistas y poetas tremendas
The next step had to be
what people couldn't stand to see
creation of *El Embassy*
Pedro blessing me
with my passport
Spanglish national anthem
and a healthy heaping
of Pietri poetry

Nothing lasts forever
So what makes poets
the exception?
He slipped away to the heavens
The view was better up there

The voice of the many disenfranchised
and though vanished into the air
never banished from our hearts
his words
his gifts
his friendship
I will never forget

Every time I take a plane
and rise above the clouds
I look for you—
not on Cloud 9—
the rent was too high
I spot you one day
on Cloud 116—
by the phone booth
Easy to find you
among the clouds
you're still wearing all black

You smile
I smile back
knowing that
I will see you soon

Pedro always had his head in the clouds
The view was better up there

ODE TO A BROTHER: BASHED BUT NOT BEATEN
Dedicated to MX

Tears form
in the bottom of my eyelids
but don't fall

Used to keep feelings to myself
at least in public
It's a man thing, I guess

When they do fall
they don't get far
my face itches
I wipe them away

Wish I was there
not sure what I could've done
I always want to save someone
as I myself fall into oblivion

Those that came after you
could've been my friends
in another life

Would I have helped?
You? Them?

Would I have kept walking,
acting like it was not my business?

Would I be as guilty of the beating
if I never laid a hand on you?

I'd like to think I would've done something
helped you
because you were a human being
not because you were my friend
I want justice
I want revenge
I want peace

I want for everything to be
the way it used to be

Could it have been me,
instead of you that day?
A different neighborhood,
different attackers,
same result?

Scars on your body
scars on your soul
and an ear that doesn't work
like it used to

I want you to hear
I want you to heal
I want it all to be okay

It's getting better
It's different
but it's not worse
than any other obstacle
in your life
just different

You are alive
for that I am thankful
to take inspiration
from the strength
the resolve
the love
of someone like you

Jason "Majestik
Originality"
Hernández

PRAY FOR ME

You call me a lost soul
and explain to me that my sins can be forgiven
tell me that God exists in me
and that all I need to do is come back

Pray For Me

Back to what?
I ask that question a million times
and receive a billion lies that I have heard a trillion times
out of the same tri-billion mouths one by one

Pray For Me

I'm told that my world can change for the better,
if I believe and follow, yet I'm told also
to believe in myself and follow no one
So whom do I listen to and whom do I hear?

Pray For Me

My beliefs are based on the actions of past factions
who came blasting with weaponry and words
called my ancestors savage and devil worshippers
Slaughtered, Raped, and Defiled in the name of their GOD
Erasing thru pain the love that was thought of as their power

Pray For Me

Allow me to confess my devotion to not follow your leader
let me be who I am and serve my spirits in the form I choose
Forgive them father, they forgot about their Orisha's
They are blind to truths because the lies have made them feel free

Pray For Me

Brushing off my beliefs and calling me atheist
they still believe I can be saved, yet I know they cannot
The only way to truly believe is to see the truth,
so I walk with eyes and ears open, saluting my siblings.

Knowing to respect how they feel and not force opinions,
such as the invaders did to our ancestors

Pray For Me

Why? Because you love me, because you believe,
because you see me as a lost soul and don't want me to die,
because I am your husband, cousin, friend, acquaintance,
emcee, poet, and all around at times a good man

Pray For Me

Because love and honor are truly what we want to die with
we don't need the truth to die happy, just thoughts.
We don't need the truth to set us free, just love.

Pray For Me

Not because I'm wrong in your eyes
but because I exist in your life as you do in mine.
Not because it's your Christian or Catholic duty
but because we are friends and family

Pray For Me

As I do for all of you in my private moments and thoughts,
as I do from my heart, because I would rather die seeing you happy.
Do not ask your maker to forgive someone he has not made
Keep me in your heart because I know I am safe there.

Pray for Love

Pray for Honor

Pray that we get to debate, joke, laugh, cry, console,
comfort, strengthen, uplift, and support each other always.
Because in that prayer, we do agree. We are eye to eye.

I See You

I Love You

Regardless of our seat assignments in the afterlife

Pray For Me

Because I will always Pray To See You in the Next

Ache

FOR HER

I have spent countless tears on a wish
hoping one day, I will see you happy
and bear witness to the creation of your smile
as it rises from the ashes of a frown once thought permanent

I long to see how long that smile will last
I ache to know you will no longer feel pain
I ponder for months about how it may be possible
about how there has to be a way to ensure the chances
of us being able to have a child

I want to find a recipe for a potion, smoothie,
milkshake, fruit, vegetable, herb, anything that
I can cook up and devour, so that my seed can help.
But I am just a man

Although I am a man, I wish to feel what you do
I yearn to carry your burden on my shoulders
to dismiss your negative thoughts about being barren
I want to hold you and infuse the jolt needed for your soul
so that you will not give up

I want you to know that although I don't know,
I wish to know, just so I could know,
what it feels like to hold the keys to your womb

I want to take away the resentment you feel on Mother's Day
I want to carry a blackjack and knockout every bad moment
when you feel you are a failure to me
I want to take the monkey off your back and prove it doesn't exist

I want to . . . no, I need to let you see how beautiful,
just how beautiful you are to me

I need you to know how happy I am because of
How much of a mother you are to my daughter
The way you accepted her into your heart
The happiness she feels when she sees you
is the same as that of a healthy biological love

You- the mother that she looks for and up to at times
when with her own, she cannot

I need you to see for yourself
that you are more than just my wife
you are more than just an expectation
you are my foundation, my backbone,
my rock, my religion, my faith, my heart,
and most importantly my soul

You yearn to become a mother
so our love can exist in a physical form
but I say you already are, because our love is like a child

Our love was like a newborn
we nurtured it, guided it along the way,
made sure it was fine when we thought it wasn't
that it felt better when we thought it was sick
and that we embraced it when it felt cold
watched it grow out of its shell into marriage
and now . . .
now we get to see our love grow old with each other

Like they say, it takes two,
and I couldn't have done it without you

I know we lost our chance of seeing our love
create itself in your womb
Miscarried because life's hands were weak

But in that lost moment, I found hope
I realized there was a way to strengthen its hands
I saw what was needed
it was to believe in what we already established
I found myself fortified in our tears
as we held each other mortified because of what happened
Life was taken away but our love wasn't
and because of that,
next time, it will hold strong and deliver
that smile I starve to see you add to the many
I haven't seen in a while

I will not allow myself to watch you decay,
when I know you are fresh in my heart
I can't promise tomorrow
but I promise my love will last until we don't

Most of all,
I promise to never give up on us becoming the family
that we wish to be

Because Family is what we already are

TOOK YOUR SEAT

It's about 5:45 in the evening
I'm tired
had a bad day at work
I'm thirsty and with no dollar to get a drink
Waiting for the N train to Canal to connect to the J
my feet hurt and the pain screams in my nerves
like a room filled with a 100 colicky babies
I begin to step side to side when finally it arrives
Now it isn't the first time that I board this ride,
so as I stand right where the door opens, towards the front of the car,
I begin to throb with excitement
my feet feel like a junkie
prepping its first hit of the day
Train begins to stop
and so does time
I look to my side and realize,
between my stress from work and the million 'lil hammers rattling
against every pressure point of my feet,
that I'm not the only one waiting for the downtown N train
So, as it screeches to a stop, the bodies come closer
compressing with anxiousness,
but it's more than anxiousness to go home,
it's the equivalent to stopping at a red light
and another car pulls up and wants a race
so I prep my mental game
gather my wits about me as my eyes scan for a seat
No, No, No, No, shit, no, no, no, no, YES!!

To my left, away in the corner right, under an ad that says,
"If you see something, say something"
So I see my seat and say YEEEESSS!
Celebrating in my thoughts as I hear the music of victory
knowing I will be able to get all this weight off of my feet
So as I make my way to the empty two seater,
which becomes my solo chair due to my 2-person posterior,
I sit and explode with excitement
happy that I get to relax
until . . . UNTIL . . .

I see the hate in your eyes!

I see the name-calling, the disgust, the snarl,
the rolling of your optics
that clearly are upset that my FAT ASS got here first
You can't stand this fat, overweight, obese,
humongous, roly-poly, gigantic, pudgy monster
Double chinned, double d having ass mother fucker
who probably sits all day dipping Twinkies in Nutella
while eating a calzone stuffed with pepperoni, sausage,
ground beef and extra cheese
and has the nerve to drink it all down with a Diet Coke
FAT FUCK!

I get to sit where any two of you could have enjoyed the ride
I hear the way you breathe, the way you sigh at the fact that
I TOOK YOUR SEAT
Your precious 'lil seat
it feels to you as if I bombarded my way into my relaxing position because I
threw my weight around,
maybe scared people with my size
and you wish you could be the hero to call me out
and make me feel ashamed for wanting the same thing you wanted before the
train got here

So I look at you directly in your eyes
all of you
and all I can think of is . . .

I'm sad that you feel like my body is so disgusting
that you wouldn't want to sit next to me
Wouldn't want to share in this feeling of joy,
knowing you have a seat for the ride
I'm sad because I don't realize the size of my left half enough
to see you wouldn't fit where I believe you could, if you tried.
It hurts me knowing that you hate me and don't even know me.
it makes me hate myself after a few minutes,
knowing that I'm not just another passenger,
but more like a freak in everyone's eyes

So I close my eyes, put my music on blast thru my headphones
and just hope that when I arrive to Canal Street,
my connecting train won't make me feel as bad as you did
Thanks for making me feel like shit

'cause in the process I forgot why I was stressed at work
and that my feet hurt, but now I just wanna go home
and forget I exist

Thank You Stranger
Sorry that I took your seat.

Myrna Nieves

THE REQUEST
to Zaadia

Translated by Chris Brandt

The naiads say
over the sea's leaden mirror
"Give us your daughter so we may comb her hair,"
their tresses long and thick
like river rushes,
their hands cold as nickel,
eyes you can look through into bottomless wells.
"No" the mother replies calmly,
"My daughter is lovely as the sun's caress
her breast is a little bird,
her laugh a brook that slakes my thirst.
I will comb my daughter's hair."
The naiads flail suspended,
their foggy garments
fill with air and billow softly,
they are of one mind,
they turn their eyes to the little girl
admire her soft skin
her innocent face.
"We'll come back for her.
She'll be happy with us.
Our realm is sublime."
The Mother keeps combing and says
"My daughter is born of my womb.
I feed her with love and with words.
She drank my blood, my milk.
I rock her to sleep at night in my arms.
I wake her with a song.
I tell you, naiads-
you may live in a realm of gold
but night and day
I'll be beside my little girl.
She belongs to my realm.
She shall inherit the Earth."

INCONFORME

Dices que no entiendes mi descontento con la realidad
que sueño demasiado y en la mañana estoy cansada
dices que no acepto la vida como es
la camuflo, la disfrazo
la hermoseo, la deformo
con mi nostalgia del porvenir
como una niña pobre de un pueblo perdido
inventando juegos a falta de juguetes
en mamparas llenas de polvo y telarañas
en casas desiertas de tíos muertos
leyendo las cartas de amor que se escribieron durante la guerra
creando intrigas y amantes en pasadizos
que huelen a orín y a salitre...
Cuando me doy cuenta que soy así,
lavo, plancho, cocino, mapeo
pero al limpiar los cristales de la ventana
exactamente la que da al baño
me acuerdo de los espejos con flamingos de los abuelos
sueño con toldos chinos, ancianos nobles, cabarets infames
Y brota de mi frente
este vientre de estrellas que heredé de mi madre

ANCIENT MEMORIES
regarding the war against Iraq
translated by Ana Betancourt

Tell me
How to greet the day
When in my heart
A somber flower is born
Fruit of the night's
Morbid gestations
Purple petaled flower
Forced to grow
By police sirens
Helicopters' helixes
News of a war

A sunny Baghdad emerges
On the edges of my dream
Baghdad with its' mosques and palaces
Baghdad of the one thousand and one nights
Magic city
Of childhood movies and tales
Ancient Mesopotamia of the Tigris and Euphrates

Today in Baghdad
The market was blown to pieces
A little girl's tiny shoes
Lay empty
Among dates, olives, and torn bodies
Today
The city is covered in blood and sand
There is a scent of uranium bullets in the air

What will be left of Nineveh and Babylon?
Of Asshur of the Assyrians and Ur of the Caldeans?
Who will gather the remains
Of the Ottoman Empire's treasures?
Who will return the statues of Innana
To the temples of Nippur?
Whose eyes will contemplate
The Ishtar Gate without weeping?
When will the legends of Gilgamesh be told anew?

I don't know,
How we keep walking up and down the street,
Eating bread in the market,
Buying meat for supper,
Walking groomed fleecy dogs.
Don't know how we didn't learn the lesson
From the ashes of the Towers.
Don't we get tired of so much war?

Could it be that my flower is born
In a remote marsh,
a lagoon
Where a dark vegetation
A fermented memory
grows?

Yet I know that in the submerged garden
Of all those that breathe in the planet
These forgotten forms exist
Beneath the unrelenting rain of rubble
Persevering in the shadows
Possessed of an inner light
That strange phosphorescence.

Let the tremulous flowers of silence arise!
Let the outcry of those of us
Who inhabit the air be heard!
Let us stop the genocide
With our actions
So that we may rescue
Our ancient cradle
So that no more bloody petals
Shall drop down to the Earth.

ANTIGUAS MEMORIAS
en torno a la guerra contra Iraq

Cómo saludar el día
cuando en el corazón nace
una flor oscura
fruto de gestaciones mórbidas
de la noche
flor de pétalos morados
crecida a fuerza
de sirenas de la policía
hélices de helicópteros
noticias de una guerra

Baghdad emerge soleada
a orillas de mi sueño
Baghdad con sus mezquitas y palacios
Baghdad de las mil y una noches
ciudad mágica
de películas y cuentos de la niñez
la Antigua Mesopotamia del Tigris y el Éufrates

Hoy en Baghdad,
el mercado ha saltado en pedazos
los pequeños zapatos de una niña
yacen vacíos entre dátiles, aceitunas
y cuerpos destrozados
hoy
la ciudad se cubre de sangre y arena
hay olor a balas de uranio en el aire

¿Qué quedará de Níniveh y Babilonia,
de Ashur de los asirios y Ur de los caldeos?
¿Quién reunirá los restos de los tesoros
del Imperio Otomano?
¿Quién devolverá las estatuas de Inana
a los templos de Nippur?
¿Qué ojos contemplarán sin llorar los portales de Ishtar?
¿Cuándo se contarán de nuevo las gestas de Gilgamesh?
No sé, cómo seguimos
caminando por la calle,
comiendo pan en el mercado,

comprando la carne de la cena,
paseando perritos lanudos y acicalados.
No sé como de los escombros de las torres
no alcanzamos a aprender la lección
¿No nos fatiga tanta guerra?

¿Será que mi flor nace
De una ciénaga remota
Donde crece una oscura vegetación
Fermento de la memoria?

Mas sé que en el sumergido jardín
De todo el que respira en el planeta
Existen estas formas olvidadas
Bajo la lluvia tenaz de los escombros
Perseverando en la sombra
Poseídas de una luz interior
Esa extraña fosforescencia.

¡Que salgan las flores aterciopeladas
del silencio!
Que se alce el clamor
de los que habitamos el aire.
Que detengamos tanto genocidio
con nuestros actos
para que rescatemos nuestra antigua cuna
Para que no caigan
más pétalos ensangrentados
sobre la Tierra.

A TALE OF LATE OCTOBER

on our way home
my daughter recoiled at the sight of the church
the daycare had a few rooms in the old building
the fall wind raised dry leaves and dust from the street
she looked slightly frightened, clutching her scarf to her face
what's the matter, mamita, I asked
-there is a witch buried in that church
beneath the floor, an old witch
nobody remembers
they do not know she is there
but I do
I looked at the steeple of the church, tall,
a black-orange needle in late October
drawn in sharp tones against the early evening sky
the street suddenly deserted
not a sound
only the dry branches swinging in the wind

we hurried home

the next Thursday
rushing from my job, I arrive early
I wait in the hall for my daughter's classes to end
I see a newspaper clipping on the board
unfair trials of witches long ago
utter ignorance about their tradition
I want to read more
the teacher comes with her
gentle, observant of my reading
my daughter smiling in front
small and trustful
against the backdrop
of her teacher's perennial black dress

the next week
the note was not there
I asked
nobody remembered

I MISS YOUR FRIENDSHIP
translated by Chris Brandt

I miss your friendship
not your kisses --
our conversations in the dark
the galleries we went to
the shared solitude
the moments of communion
over a news story, a book
a painting.
I miss your friendship.
One time you said
why don't we get married
again
and when I asked why
you said
I don't get along with anyone
only with you.

Today, facing a cold, rainy
spring day
I understand
that nothing will rub away
the mark of Cain on my
forehead,
stigma of solitude
that I confused with hunger,
nothing will hold back
the silent crash
of an ancestral ocean
that breaks in my breast
and the fleeting curve of an image
a stroke of an unexpected color
the sudden dread of this interior
labyrinth
where you tried to enter
your curious face
those are my only possession
the traces which I bear
--wounded and proud--
of this expulsion from paradise

NOTES FOR A POEM OF MID-NOVEMBER

Orchard Beach lies serenely in a cool November afternoon: splendid sky, splendid sea. We walk, carefree. The boardwalk is a path to the sandy shore. In the middle, lies the sculpture of a huge swan. I wonder who put it there. Then the elegant neck moves. It's alive! What is this creature doing in Orchard Beach? The waves continue to bathe the shore. A few people walk around. An old woman pays attention and gets closer. The swan, nervous, agitates its feathers lightly, but it hardly moves. It goes back to its statuesque pose of exquisite lines. I move closer and look casually, trying not to scare it. My lover walks briskly ahead, uncomfortable by the scene. "It must be sick, this is definitely not its element"- he says. I look again and the beak is wet; some liquid--possibly an infection—runs down. Yet the animal sits with great dignity; a rare view over the wood: a swan in Orchard Beach.

I look back to delight in its form. We humans are so different: short, tall, fat, thin, have big or small heads, and the swan is just an unblemished silhouette, pure form. "We are more interesting"—my lover says, but I am captivated by its outstanding beauty. We continue walking and the rocks are calling us to sit and watch the waters. I look for shells in the sand. They are all broken, even a plastic spoon tricks me. "This afternoon I am looking for perfection"—I say.

The day grows cooler on the rocks. We take the road back and the swan is not there. I look around. Did it fly away or was it picked up? I watch the sea quietly bathing the shore and think that I will always remember this day: the sand, my lover's hands, and the magnificent swan in its wounded perfection.

Tito Luna

HERITAGE PIECE (INDIO)

I am Mayan
I'm the reincarnation of a lost civilization
that buried its roots deep inside the womb of women
such as my Salvadorian grandmother
Yo soy azteca
hijo del sol Mexicano
piel cultivada en tierra de guerreros
cultura de sacrificio y siempre listo pa' la batalla
I'm a hybrid
50-50
so I possess mathematics in my fingertips
2012 doesn't scare me
'cuz I already know human greed already has us doomed
I carry the curse of Monte Suma in my words
so I spit it out knowing my daughter will one day do the same
I take jaguar steps
and walk with the Mayan visionary serpent on my arm
there's no moon pyramids wall around my mind
so I run Sun God stone circles around these fools
with my modern day hieroglyphics
sacrificial rituals lying dormant beneath the surface of my skin
the right of passage has already been tattooed
into the ancestral spirits I have within
I'm the reincarnation of 2 civilizations that burned their roots deep
within my elders
and now transcends me

MR. FLORES

Take a look around
the odor of death floats and lingers around the corner
u can smell the medication in the air
as it comes out of human pores
there is no righteousness left here
just a prayer, left to be answered
in a moment of desperation
So, how many doctors does it take
to get to the bottom of his medical problems?
1 . . . 2 . . . 3 . . .
Mr. Flores will never know
he knows that he is dying
he tells me, "Papi, I feel it. I don't give a fuck no mo.
I have no more life in me."
and doctors reply with words
that the devil him self wouldn't condone
"Well, Mr. Flores, you have lived a long life"
A long life!
As I hear this, I feel tears building inside of me,
but I can't nor will cry in front of this man
to think that 52 is a long life
my eyes have witnessed the slow internal destruction of a man struck by a
sickness that won't be cured this time around
his legs are as big as my arms
he is nothing but skin and bone
5'8" weighing in at 122 pounds
something u would see on old photographs
of Nazi concentration camps
the lack of natural sun light
seems to have damaged his melanin
causing his brown Puerto Rican skin to look pale
like the paint on a vintage car
way past the point of buffering
and too old to bring back the shine
what used to be thick black hair dark like a wild forest
has been decimated to thinned out fibers
that now looks more like infertile soil
his cheek bones are prominent- the lack of fatty tissue
And the muscle on his face lets his eyes do most of the explaining he knows
that he's a dead man talking

and still, he manages to squeeze a laugh here and there accompanied by a story
of the good old days
"Oye papi, I remember cuando el barrio era el barrio. We used ta party all
night and all morning if we could. Oye papi, tu ves esa enfermera aya? Esa
nurse, she wants me, papi. She wants to jump my bones and I think i ma let
her!" he laughs
We laugh as he knows, deep in his heart,
at this point in his life, he doesn't even want himself
with salsa running through his veins
and Puerto Rican pride in his heart
he's a throw back to the few O.G.'s left over
from the old school of el barrio
even with his 'fuck-you-attitude'
he is now fragile
too weak to stand
Yet too hard-headed to stop trying
he's in need of conversation
for the lack of family that stop by to pay a visit
He tells me, "Papi, ju know a lot of us from that era are dead. I guess I should
be lucky to make it to 52. Most of my friends died from drugs ju know, OD'd
on that good shit from back in the days. What they sell now in the streets is
mierda papi, mierda! Some of them got shot, stabbed, killed or that AIDS got
us. You know, 'the monsta!'"
He talks as if he is the last of his kind
the last of an endangered species
"Man, I had some good times at The Copa- a lot of woman, fine woman
too. Shiiitt! I used ta pull them in just like this!" fast snapping motion with
his hand, "Wha? Ju don't believe me? I wasn't always like this. I was good
looking. Ju know, suave!"
Even in this state, he holds on to his sanity
I guess no one wants to talk about how they are dying
when they are dying . . . but about how they lived
so I tell him, "What you need to do is get outta here, pa! Go to PR and just
chill! Set up a hammock between two coconut trees and have a Corona right
by the beach with a good-looking woman!"
He answered, "I should, right papi? I should right?"
and for a minute, he got stuck in a daydream
made him look as if he had some of that heroin in his veins
Then he continued, "But there's nothing for me in Puerto Rico, papi.
Nothing! I was born here. I'm a Nuyorican. Yo soy de Nueva York!"
wondering how long I could keep a straight face
while looking at the shell of a man

that I have seen walking in and out of the hospital
the last two and a half years
Now in front of me, Mr. Flores lays in ICU bed 3
2009 December 25 at 930 in the morning
and I'm thinking, "What a way to spend the holidays!" surrounded but IV's,
vent machines, trek tubes,
heart monitors, contact isolation,
and other patients whose future looks dimmer then his own
I see it in his eyes
he is no longer scared of his outcome
weak and beaten
grateful for the life he has gotten to live
with salsa in his veins
and Puerto Rican pride in his heart
He's a throw back to the few O.G.'s
left from the old school of el barrio
an endangered species
maybe the last of his kind
Mr. Flores, que Dios te bendiga
God bless you
Y pa' lante papi
pa' lante

SPIC

Let me write what I think . . .
I think loneliness and desperation, most of the time,
Can become a transformation of negative energy
into a form of inspiration
For the time being,
I think my thoughts need liberation
So out loud I think
I think out loud
Out loud I think
I think . . .
People need to stop thinking
that illegal Latinos need to vanish back to their countries
Not recognizing that it's not by choice
but because necessity drives them to come here
That in all reality, most of the jobs my people get
The regular American citizen with working papers
wouldn't work for
So stop saying that immigrants are stealing your jobs
If we were to vanish what would happen to Americas agriculture?
In California, who would pick fruits one by one?
In Florida, who would work the orange fields?
Let me tell you something
I think a lot of people's gardens, lawns, and trees
would not get trimmed
Look at the big picture
Who would work at the fast food restaurants?
Who would wash dishes at the five star restaurants? Period.
If it wasn't for the immigrant's children born in this land
America's troops would dwindle down dramatically
Look at the big picture
Think about the car washes, all the bodegas,
all the Latino TV channels
'Cause at one point
everyone has tried to watch a Hispanic soap opera
Or, as we call them, novelas
Think about the low-rider car shows
Even some of the Chinese food spots
Think about the delivery man from your nearest pizza spot
No more Feliz Navidad,
No more Tony Montana

Texas, California, Florida, New York, Arizona,
Ohio, New Mexico, Colorado
would be all somewhat empty
And so would Nevada!
WE'RE EVERYWHERE!
Fucking just EVERYWHERE!
We're in New York City, Brooklyn, Queens, Long Island,
the Bronx, Staten Island and Yonkers
We're in Nassau County, Rikers Island, Upstate, Pelican Bay
and a maximum penitentiary somewhere down in Alabama
You can catch us in your nearest barber shop,
Laundromat, the nearest boys and girls club
You can catch us in the subway system, buses, taxis
Shit we are that taxi driver, so what?
We do everything from Cablevision to superstition
From announcing:
Goooooooooooooooooooooooooooooooooaaaaaaaaaaaaal!
To yelling, "Hell no, I ain't paying no child support!"
as we walk out of family court
We have no need for passports because once we're here,
guess what?
That's right- we don't travel much
If it wasn't for us, Western Union would simply go bankrupt
Because we're the ones sending most of the money
to other countries
Get it through your thick skull
WE'RE EVERYWHERE!
Fucking just EVERYWHERE!
So unless you don't like Latina women with their Latina curves
Latino men with their Latino friends
Miami Beach, Spanish Harlem, that yeyo or that sticky icky green
Along with the Salvadorian, Colombian,
Mexican, Dominican and Puerto Rican day parade
Don't say shit, don't say nothing
You know we bring Sazón to America's table
And the next time you see someone
that looks somewhat Hispanic
Tell yourself you're just not able to escape us
Why?
That's right
Because WE'RE EVERYWHERE!
We're even in the same struggle that you are in

And that's the shit that makes me mad
Because if we wasn't, we wouldn't see each other
Walking on the same fucking street
Riding the same public transportation
Hearing the same warrior cries
But we're just considered immigrants
Like if you're not Native American you're not one too
Fuck the fuck outta here with that shit!
Your ignorance is more than bliss
Your ignorance can suck my dick
So I can cum on your stupidity
Hoping that the little bit of intelligence you got would choke on it
And yes, I write all of my shit
So if you have any problem with this
Take it up with the man that called me a SPIC!

Carlos Andrés Gómez

WHO WON'T BEND
for Rodrigo and his brother
"Preferible morir de pie, antes que vivir arrodillado." - Che Guevara

The scariest part for him was the idea
that his word would never be
enough. Whatever the circumstance, no man
of color's alibi can ever be perfect enough, indicted
by either rage or resignation.

Never airtight until the coffin
is sealed. Secrets buried
in an almost living man's lips, a
slave uprising grimaced into the expression
of a frozen face.

For quite a while now

the habit has been to keep the caskets
closed.

As if the mothers
are not Mamie Till. As if the crime
is any different.

Seven years ago, my friend Cynthia's cousin
was shot in the head by a state trooper
on the side of the highway during
a routine traffic stop.

He was 15.

Had just arrived from Puerto Rico the day
before. Didn't speak a word of English. Happened
to be rolling down his window.

Demons can't touch the anger in me
right now. Every time someone I know,
someone I love realizes
the coin flip that their life
is.

The common theme is kneeling,
always. To make a man
be the boy he was trained to be.

In defense of the principle:

destroy what is beautiful to justify
the blank canvas of authority, the drunk
card game of it all.

Before I was born, when my friend Piseth's dad
was stopped one day by the Khmer Rouge in Cambodia,
the men gave his father a choice:
One at the head or two at the feet –
a single bullet left in the chamber
and spun.

Luckily,
he picked right, learned
the hefty price of playing the game:
survival.

He still walks with a limp
like
all the black and brown men
in my neighborhood, shiny shackles
around their necks, an almost Till-ing,
laughing through teeth smuggling gold
stained with ghosts.

VITRUVIUS
for the young men on Rikers Island

We are architects of creation and of destruction
but men are from Mars so we plot for war. Enslave

geniuses to develop atom bombs and clone sheep,
what else can you expect from us?

When we use proofs on inner-city kindergarteners to
determine how many jail cells to build?

When we place numerical value on everything from eyesight
to unemployment to letting an undocumented person die?

When we throw prison sentences around the ghettos like humanitarian aid rice
during food ration days at a refugee camp?

How could you expect that we not be obsessed with math? Compulsive in
our space and time addiction, flaunt ourselves as complex, compared symbols,
never simplified. We are all just derivatives.

What is the measure of a man?

I see men on my street holding their sons' hands, walk the block
like they're going to war. Fingers crossing paths like an X and
Y axis, like a mother and son army base good-bye. Afraid that
they might be buried alive for showing how much they care.

We care so much sometimes as men; we lash out and throw punches
at the air. Sometimes so broken by it we play up big dick paradigms
even though we know they cancel out our human variable. Simplify
us into nothing more than a violent, sexually-loaded word problem,
but at least we're in someone's notebook.
More than: a victim, we think,
more than: another guy in a faded lacrosse hat
or an oversized bright white T,
more than: a man we never knew but wanted to,
more than: the less than we're so used to,
saying to myself,
I'll be anybody as long as it's not nobody
I'll be anybody as long as it's not nobody.

What is the measure of a man?

I think of Leonardo Da Vinci's Vitruvian Man
his sketched proportions of a man trying to fly, trapped
in a square trapped in a circle. Why are we always trying
to box in the creative, ascending miracle of what we are?

We are so much more than the ungraceful, scalene dimensions, obtuse-angled
mechanical emblems we exchange for love, but more men of color know
the shadows cast by prison cell right angles than the sunlight of transparent
squares in dorm rooms, more immigrant men know the flat steel paneling of
truck trailer's four walls than the open air of owning their own yard, we go to
war and come back in blue, white, and red-cloaked rectangles, stacked into the
circular hull of a flying midnight ship whose only trick is being able to invert
parabolas.

We are more than the geometric lines prescribed to us as children.

Erase the square, paint over the circle, Leonardo, stop trying
to quantify who he is and let your Vitruvian Man live. Let him
break out and just show you. Can't you see that both his arms and legs are still
moving?

Release him, Leonardo, so we can show you Vitruvius. Show you
that we are more than what we are merely worth. Show you every-
thing that we are.

INHERITANCE

I.
It is utterly frantic, indescribable to remember
your mother's birthday two hours and seventeen
minutes after it has passed.

Gag reflex like a rusty slowly-pulled trigger, bile
churned and bubbling.

II.
I sent a seventy-five dollar bouquet
rush delivery, brushed away the cold
sweat and took a shower.

III.
My mother seemed distracted at dinner,
and then,
Carlos, I know you forgot my birthday
and it's okay. I only bring it up because
I'm scared that if I didn't you might always
think that you can get away with it, like
your father.

IV.
Love at its best is a brisk slap in the face.

The unflinching reflex of a parent
as you dash towards the busy street
in front of your house.

A shocked regret rustling through
that parent's hard fought stoicism
as your lip drools red, your petrified
body stiff with surprise.

Parenthood at its best is a heavy weapon:
able to protect and to kill.

Each swing impossible to take back.

A fiery molded iron carving

leeches from the backs of babies

or a smoking revolver
seemingly aimed at your head,
as some dangerous ghost just behind you
tumbles to the floor.

ZOO

The contradiction of it all
has never quite resolved itself:
self-professed animal lovers
visiting animals in cages

a polar bear masturbating intermittently
as the tranquilizers wear thin, like the sky
blue paint she licks to the concrete bone,
confused by the heated ice petrified to stone

yesterday I'm in the mote
pretending like I'm not one of the idiots
that got caught, flanked on all sides
by gazelles in tutus, caked makeup
faces like a spray-painted flamingo
at the Bronx Zoo, their infinite stork
legs like red woods about to be toppled
to the ground to build condominiums

the lot of animals we are is mostly fresh
meat, only a handful of lions drooling toothless
against the thick, reinforced glass while bratty
little rug rats tap against their faces and shine laser
pointers under their eyelids, no one learns their lesson
these days

graceful sweeping strides captivate the non-
existent peanut gallery each of us has imagined,
a thousand True Hollywood Stories simultaneously
being taped

every exchange is a false revelation, an aged
loaf of bread so stale that the dentures crack
on its diamond skin, all competing to be the best
juggling monkey

each person more aware of the other than ever
yet utterly invisible.

ILLUSIONIST
for Pho (Ban Luang, Thailand 1999)

I thought he had an
unfair advantage

three fingers to my five

his awkward hand seemingly made
for the yo-yo's
otherworldly science

the quantum mechanics
of teasing something out
fully
and completely

then,
swallowing it all
back to the source
and making it vanish

that small arm like a wand

his gaping cleft palate,
an unpeeling of his upper lip
like a raw flower
thirsty to share its
unfinished beauty

the American factory upstream
had turned their drinking water
to sorcerous potion

it allowed him to pull off unthinkable feats
I could only marvel at

the constant telekinetics of his arthritic paws

his rare trick of turning yellow
in the hospital,
laughing more than he usually did

when I visited,

the I.V. in his arm
flooding his veins
with lead

the stomach tumors, twisting miracles
like balloon animals at a surprise
birthday party

and then he disappeared

three days later,
the sheets changed
his clothes folded up,

like he was never there.

Sufridas, 2010
Mixed media collage

AUTHOR BIOGRAPHIES

EDWIN TORRES was born in El Bronx to citizens of a Puerto Rican flavor, Isabel Gonzalez & Felipe Torres. Recipient of numerous awards in the poetric landscape, he's arrived from planet Noricua to collaborate with the universal diaspora. He's the author of 7 books, including *Yes Thing No Thing* (Roof Books), *In the Function of External Circumstances* (Nightboat Books), *The PoPedology of an Ambient Language* (Atelos Books), and *The All-Union Day of the Shock Worker* (Roof Books).

RIGOBERTO GONZÁLEZ is the author of eight books, most recently of the young adult novel, *The Mariposa Club*, and a story collection, *Men without Bliss*. He also edited the anthology *Camino del Sol: Fifteen Years of Latina and Latino Writing*. The recipient of Guggenheim and NEA fellowships, winner of the American Book Award, and The Poetry Center Book Award, he writes a Latino book column for the *El Paso Times* of Texas. He is contributing editor for *Poets and Writers Magazine*, on the Board of Directors of the National Book Critics Circle, and is Associate Professor of English at Rutgers—Newark, State University of New Jersey.

MARIA RODRIGUEZ-MORALES is a Brooklyn born Nuyorican poet and published writer. She has performed at the Nuyorican Poets Cafe, The Bowery Poetry Club, Preguntas Arts Cafe, and many other venues in the Metro area. A member of the NYC Latina Writers Group, she also facilitates a poetry workshop and open mic for inner city youth at the South Queens Boys and Girls Club. Maria is a married mother of four boys.

ERIK "ADVOCATE OF WORDZ" MALDONADO, a founding member of El Grito de Poetas, rips them all- papers, stages, microphones, and unfair parking tickets. This Bronx native's bold and diverse tongue has toured theatres and universities for nearly a decade now, as well as curated various spoken word workshops. He featured at the world renowned Lincoln Center as part of their Meet the Artist series, hosted the Open Room at the legendary Nuyorican Poets Cafe, and is a veteran cast member of the Lose Control comedy troupe. He also hosts The Inspired Word Poetry Readings and is the creator of HipHopPoetry.com, which PBS has included in lesson plans for teachers abroad. His work can be found in various publications and he has an affinity for not wasting people's time and avoiding the predictable.

BONAFIDE ROJAS is a poet, musician, and author of *"pelo bueno" a day in the life of a nuyorican poet* (dark souls press, 2005). He is the bandleader for The Mona Passage, the 2002 Louder Arts Slam This! Champion, has appeared on "Def

Poetry Jam," has been published in the anthologies: *Bum Rush The Page: a def poetry jam, Role Call, Learn Then Burn, Centro Journal, Hostos Review, Calabash Journal, The Acentos Review* and has performed across the United States. He prefers black chuck taylors, loves The Beatles & New York City.

LUZMA UMPIERRE is a poet, educator, and human rights advocate; born in Santurce, Puerto Rico, where she graduated with honors from both the Sacred Heart Academy and the Sacred Heart University. In 1974, Umpierre came to reside in the United States. She has published several books, including *Una puertorriqueña en Penna, En el país de las maravillas, The Margarita Poems,* and over 100 articles, among them, "La ansiedad de la influencia en Sandra María Estévez y Marjorie Agosín," published in the anthology *Woman of Her Word: Hispanic Women Write.* Umpierre has undertaken legal battles and pioneering work for the inclusion of issues of sexual orientation, gender, race, class, and ethnicity in the curriculum of universities. She also helped found and worked for The Pennsylvania Association for Bilingual Education and the International Classroom at the University of Pennsylvania to help Latina/o children be given proper educational rights in the state's school system. In 2004, the MLA held an homage session at their yearly convention to honor Dr. Umpierre's poetry and humanitarian work. She received a Lifetime Achievement Award in 1990 from the Gay and Lesbian organizations of New Jersey. She has also received awards for her advocacy of AIDS patients, including the Bayard Rustin Award from AIDS Massachusetts and Woman of the Year at Western Kentucky University. Umpierre was named Outstanding Woman of Maine by the USA Congress in 2002. Umpierre received her Ph.D. from Bryn Mawr College, PA. She now resides in Florida.

PAUL S. FLORES is a prominent spoken word performer, playwright, and professor who continues to influence a new generation of Latino artists through his work exploring the intersection of urban culture, Hip-Hop, Spanglish and transnational identity. Raised in Chula Vista, CA, and based in San Francisco, Flores' performance projects have taken him from HBO's *Def Poetry* to Havana, Cuba, Mexico City, and El Salvador. He is author of the novel *Along the Border Lies,* and his most recent play REPRESENTA! was directed by Danny Hoch and presented by the Hip-Hop Theater Festival 2007.

ROBERTO "SIMPLY ROB" VASSILARAKIS, a founding member of El Grito de Poetas, is a born and raised New Yorker of Greek and El Salvadoran descent. Disowned at the age of 17 for being gay, he was forced to leave his mama's boy life behind. Taking to the streets and learning how to fend for himself paved the road for his spoken word journey with concrete inspiration. His life experience led him to dedicate himself to working with the "at risk" inner city youth of NYC focusing on issues of sex/sexual identity and HIV/AIDS prevention and education. He has been blessed to work with many LGBT adolescents, their straight counterparts, and those who might be questioning.

CARIDAD DE LA LUZ "LA BRUJA" is a Bronx-born poet/actor/activist considered one of America's leading spoken word artists. She is a renaissance woman. *The New York Times* called her "a Juggernaut" after her 2009 run of her musical "Boogie Rican Blvd." at the Puerto Rican Traveling Theater. Her music crossed over internationally with her debut album, *Brujalicious*, available on iTunes and she captivated audiences with her performance on *Russell Simmons presents Def Poetry* on HBO. She is the Founder of the Latinas 4 Life movement and is a Board member of Voices UnBroken. She believes the power of word helps create positive change in the lives of countless inner-city youth and has taught poetry workshops for over 13 years to help build a foundation for self-expression and empowerment. Her new album, *For Witch It Stands*, is available for download on iTunes

EMANUEL XAVIER was born and raised in New York City and survived the streets as an underage hustler and drug dealer to eventually reinvent himself as one of the most successful voices to emerge from the spoken word poetry movement. Of Ecuadorian and Puerto Rican descent, he is author of the novel, *Christ Like*, the poetry collection, *If Jesus Were Gay & other poems*, and, besides this anthology, he is editor of *Bullets & Butterflies: queer spoken word poetry* and *Mariposas: A Modern Anthology of Queer Latino Poetry*. He has appeared on *Russell Simmons presents Def Poetry* and his spoken word/music collaboration album with producer El David, *Legendary*, inspired a staged modern dance presentation by choreographer Ferdinand De Jesus. The title track from the album became an underground house music classic, which spawned a video helmed by French film director Arié Ohayon. The Equality Forum recently proclaimed him a GLBT Icon for his dedication to gay rights, queer homeless youth, and as an AIDS activist. He curated El Museo del Barrio's Speak Up! spoken word poetry series and continues to perform regularly throughout the country and abroad. www.emanuelxavier.com

NANCY MERCADO has a doctoral degree from Binghamton University-SUNY. She is the author of *It Concerns the Madness* and editor of *if the world were mine*, a children's anthology published by the New Jersey Performing Arts Center. Her work appears in numerous anthologies of both poetry and fiction. Nancy is the author of seven plays (one co-written with Pedro Pietri) and was an editor of *Long Shot magazine* for 11 years. She was featured along with such eminent writers as Toni Morrison and Alice Walker in the documentary film, *Yari Yari Pamberi: Black Women Writers Dissecting Globalization* directed by Jayne Cortez.

Nancy was also profiled as "one of the most celebrated Puerto Rican literary figures in New York City" in *Latino Leaders Magazine*. Her biography appears in the *Encyclopedia of Hispanic American Literature* published by Facts on File. Nancy has presented her work throughout the US, in Europe and Canada as a featured poet and conference panelist.

URAYOÁN NOEL was born and raised in San Juan, Puerto Rico, and is the author of three books of poetry: the artist's book *Las flores del mall*; *Kool Logic / La lógica kool* (Bilingual Press); and *Boringkén* (Ediciones Callejón). A contributing editor of *Mandorla*, a board member of Acentos, and a founding member of Spanic Attack, his creative and critical writings have appeared in *Contemporary Literature, Fence,* and *eXchanges: Journal of Literary Translation*. He is currently completing a book on Nuyorican poetry from the 1960s to the present, and is Assistant Professor of English at the University at Albany, SUNY, where he collaborates on the online journal *Barzakh*.

CHRIS "CHILO" CAJIGAS originally hails from Riverhead, Strong Island, New York and as a licensed History teacher, he currently educates youth in the Bronx and Brooklyn. He has been featured on numerous audio projects, mix tapes, and events, and is former member of the hip hop/spoken word group, 21 Poetz, and a founding member of one of El Grito De Poetas, who received an award in 2009 from the state department of health for their work within the HIV community. He is also half of the hip-hop group, Dr. Loco, whose album, *Lab Experiments*, can be found on iTunes. Chilo recently completed working on the Puerto Rican Freedom Project, www.prfreedomproject.org, and is currently working on a plethora of other powerful projects. A cultured and spiritual educator, Chilo enjoys giving back to the community and being part of unique collectives that can offer a multitude of beneficial services to the societies we live in today.

LATASHA N. NEVADA DIGGS is a writer, vocalist, and sound artist. She is the author of three chapbooks, *Ichi-Ban* and *Ni-Ban* (MOH Press); *Manuel is destroying my bathroom* (Belladonna Press), and the album, *Television*. Her work has been published in Rattapallax, Black Renaissance Noir, Nocturnes, Spoken Word Revolution Redux, The Black Scholar, P.M.S, Jubilat, Everything But the Burden, and Muck Works to name a few. As a vocalist and poet, she has worked with many artists including Vernon Reid, Akilah Oliver, Mike Ladd, Butch Morris, Gabri Christa, Ali Jackson, Shelley Hirsch, Burnt Sugar, Edwin Torres, Elliot Sharp, Mendi + Keith Obadike, Bernard Lang, Vijay Iyer, Ryuichi Sakamoto, Towa Tei, and Guillermo E. Brown. She has received scholarships, residencies, and fellowships from Cave Canem, Harvestworks Digital Media Arts Center, Naropa Institute, Caldera Arts, New York Foundation for the Arts (2003/2009), the Eben Demarest Trust, Harlem Community Arts Fund, Barbara Deming

Memorial Grant for Women and Lower Manhattan Cultural Council. As an independent curator and director, Latasha has produced several events with The Black Rock Coalition Orchestra. A native of Harlem, Latasha is a 2010 Pocantico Writer in Residence and a 2010 VCCA Writer in Residence.

ROBERTO F. SANTIAGO writes placing pen to paper and fingertips to QWERTY as an act of translation. Within poetry, he has discovered a booming collective of voices and a rickety soapbox for his multiple identities whereupon he can shout obscenities and prayers at the same time. Since receiving his BA from Sarah Lawrence College in Poetry and Performance Studies, Roberto has worked with the Asian Pacific Islander Coalition on HIV/AIDS (APICHA) as a community health educator and intergroup dialogue facilitator. It is in this position that he has come to understand the healing power of words. Roberto also writes and produces music, and has been known to dance until he rips his pants. He is a New Yorican Bronx-native who has accumulated over twenty addresses to date and will begin working towards his MFA at Rutgers Fall ' 10.

FRANK PEREZ was born in El Barrio and raised in El Bronx. He is a produced playwright, Obie award winning director, published author, activist, and poet. He has conducted writing/poetry workshops with the children of Vieques and worked as a teaching artist for various organizations teaching poetry/playwriting throughout the public school and penal system in the tri-state area. As a director, he directed Pedro Pietri's "El Livingroom" at the Nuyorican Poets Cafe and "Come In, We're Closed" at the New Dramatists Theater. He also directed "El Cano/The Blonde Man" by Louis Delgado for Repertorio Español, which won him an Obie award. As a playwright, Frank's productions include "Special People of International Character" (SPIC), "Next Stop: Suburbia", "Abuelita/ Granma", "Living for Yesterday", "Apostles of the Apocalypse", and "Death of a Dream" among others. His play "Special People of International Character" was published in the anthology *Action: The Nuyorican Poets Café Theater Festival.* Frank is also a published author having written the biographies of Puerto Rican actor, Raul Julia, and Mexican activist, Dolores Huerta, for the Steck-Vaughn publishing series, *Contemporary Hispanic Americans.* As a producer, he co-produced the award winning independent feature "Up With Me" and he produces a bi-weekly cable TV show called "EHTV" East Harlem Television for Manhattan Neighborhood Network.

SHEILA MALDONADO is a lifelong writer and native New Yorker. She grew up in Coney Island between Surf and Mermaid Avenues, across the street from the Atlantic Ocean. Her family is still there when they are not in their house in Honduras. She is now an amateur Mayanist, an occasional backup singer in a Latin music school band, and president and sole member of the Björk

Fan Club, Washington Heights Chapter. Her poems have been published in *Callaloo, Meridians, Rattapallax, Live Mag!* and *Stretching Panties*, as well as online at *The Acentos Review*. She teaches creative writing in NYC public schools through Teachers & Writers Collaborative and writes most on the train uptown.

JOHN "CHANCE" ACEVEDO of El Grito de Poetas has been reciting and hosting for about a decade. As the eldest of three, he receives inspiration from everyday life situations and most commonly uses a blend of comedy and drama to reflect his real-life experiences. Chance has facilitated workshops and been a featured performer at poetry venues and universities throughout the country. He has been the popular host of Brain Damage- Youth Open Mic, Microphone Fiends, and Urban Voices Heard- monthly showcases which he co-curates. Chance also hosted The First Annual New York Hip-Hop Dance Convention at Sony Studios. He has been published in *The Company We Keep* edited by Raul Maldonado and the Park Slope Poetry Project's *Erato*. Chance is founding member of the hardest working poetry troupe on the scene, El Grito de Poetas, a collective of diverse Latino and Latina poets dedicated to the craft and performance of modern poetry.

MACHETE MOVEMENT, a NY/NJ based group, was born from the creative mind of El David. Machete Movement's versatility, skill, and passion are greatly influenced by its member's musical talents and diverse musical backgrounds. Machete Movement's sound transgresses all boundaries and reaches a diverse audience ranging from hip-hop/spoken word lovers to traditional Bomba/Rumba supporters. Machete Movement includes Noel "El David" Rodriguez, Carlos Cartagena, Scott "Sever" Bell, Alex Machete, Ellen Lopez-Velez, Antonio Guttierrez, and Selina "60 Sadie" Rodriguez. Machete Movement's diverse members and mastery in a wide range of music creates a unique sound that is full of soul and culture, which celebrates what it means to be Latino and a child of latin sounds, soul, funk, and hip-hop.

LISA ALVARADO is an educator, poet, novelist, and journalist. She is the founder of La Onda Negra Press, and is author of *Reclamo* and *The Housekeeper's Diary*, originally a book of poetry and now a one-woman performance. Her first novel, *Sister Chicas* (written with Ann Hagman Cardinal and Jane Alberdeston) was bought by Penguin/NAL, and released in April 2006. *Sister Chicas* is a coming of age story concerning the lives of three young Latinas living in Chicago. *Sister Chicas* won 2nd place Best First Novel in English (Latino Literacy Now/2007). Her book of poetry, *Raw Silk Suture*, is the newest release by Floricanto Press. She has curated multimedia exhibits and mounted her own multimedia piece, *Reclamo*, in the Pilsen art corridor in Chicago; and is currently a contributor to the nationally touring exhibit, Re-imagining the Distaff Toolkit, curated by

Ricki Solinger/SUNY. Lisa is the recipient of grants from the Department of Cultural Affairs, The NEA, and the Ragdale Foundation.

A. B. LUGO is an actor, poet, and playwright. As a poet, he has performed at colleges, theater spaces, and poetry cafés throughout the United States and Puerto Rico. He appeared in a clip reciting his poetry at the Nuyorican Poets' Café on BET's "Teen Summit" (featuring Saul Williams). He is the 2006 House of Xavier Glam Slam poetry champion. His work has been published in the literary journals *99% More Free, Roots and Culture* (published by Columbia University), *The Smokin' Word* (Issue 5) and *Suspect Thoughts: a Journal of Subversive Writing* (Issue 19). As a playwright, his work has been produced in New York, New Jersey, North Carolina, and Puerto Rico. His stage play, *Banjee*, was selected as part of a college course syllabus at Michigan State University.

JASON "MAJESTIK ORIGINALITY" HERNANDEZ was born and raised in New York City. Growing up with emotionally and physically abusive parents, the music of Run DMC, Rakim, the Beastie Boys, Kool Moe Dee, and Slick Rick provided his escape. Majestik began writing poetry at the age of twelve and lyrics at fifteen. Majestik joined a group of emcees and poets known as 21 Poetz and eventually joined El Grito de Poetas in 2005. Majestik Originality has performed at various venues such as the renowned Nuyorican Poetry Club, Bowery Poetry Club, Roseland, Webster Hall, Oxygen Lounge, 718 Lounge, Colgate University, and Eastern Correctional.

MYRNA NIEVES is a writer, cultural activist, and educator. A founding member and professor at Boricua College, she was director for twenty years of its Winter Poetry Series. Published works include *Libreta de sueños (narraciones)* (1997) and *Viaje a la lluvia, poemas* (2003). She is co-author/co-editor of the collection of poetry and prose *Tripartita: Earth, Dreams, Powers* (1990), the anthology *Mujeres como islas* (2002), and the literary publications *Lugar sin límite* (1978), *Guaíza* (1986) and *Moradalsur* (2000). She produced and performed in *Directory of Dreams*, a dramatization of her narrative for the Nuyorican Poets Café (1999). Her work has been included in many literary journals and internet magazines, such as *The Poetry Project, And Then, Brújula-Compass, Red y Acción, Letras salvajes,* and *The Gathering of the Tribes*. Nieves was also selected for "The Latina Poets Festival" of the Puerto Rican Traveling Theater (2007) and many literary festivals/performances. Nieves earned a BA in World Literature at the University of Puerto Rico (Magna Cum Laude), a MA in Spanish at Columbia University, and a Ph.D. in Latin American and Caribbean Literature at New York University.

TITO LUNA was born to Salvadorian and Mexican immigrant parents in Los

Angeles, California. Raised by his mother and his grandmother, Tito's family was forced to move from place to place, eventually settling in New York. This itinerant life made Tito realize that home was not a place, but a state of mind. His poetry is his therapy, something that has not changed to this day. Tito now uses his experiences to conduct workshops for middle and high school students. Tito's voice is that of the poor, of the immigrant's struggle, his words are from the heart and every performance is one that is delivered right from his soul. He is a member of El Grito de Poetas.

CARLOS ANDRÉS GÓMEZ is an actor, playwright, and poet from New York City. He is a Russell Simmons HBO *Def Poet* and 2006 International Poetry Slam Champion. Winner of the 2009 Artist of the Year Award at the Promoting Outstanding Writers Awards, he stars in Spike Lee's #1 box office smash hit film, *Inside Man,* with a lead role alongside Denzel Washington, Jodie Foster, and Clive Owen. In the past year, he's collaborated with Tony Award-winning tap dance legend Savion Glover on Broadway, represented the United States at the Poetry Africa International Festival in Durban, South Africa, and was a special guest performer at the Macy's Passport Fashion Show. He just wrapped his 50-date Majority of One National College Tour in the spring and released his 3rd album, "Vitruvius," during the summer. For more info, please visit: www.CarlosLive.com

Oye, 2010
Mixed media collage

Breinigsville, PA USA
05 April 2011
259199BV00001B/5/P